DATE DUE

POWER
and

edited by

WILLIAM V. D'ANTONIO and HOWARD J. EHRLICH

DEMOCRACY
in AMERICA

PETER F. DRUCKER

DELBERT C. MILLER

ROBERT A. DAHL

UNIVERSITY OF NOTRE DAME PRESS • 1961

To

LORRAINE AND CAROL

"I have solved practically all the pressing questions of our time, but they keep on being propounded as insoluble just as if I never existed."

GEORGE BERNARD SHAW

Foreword

We presently are witnessing searching reappraisals of salient American values as to their prospects for fullfillment within the context of an increasingly complex society. Over the past decade a relatively new literature on the character and problems of American life has burgeoned forth—both domestically and internationally. It includes critical essays on the apparent disparities between cultural ideals and actual patterns, challenging reports to the nation concerning the need to set a clear priority of goals for the second half of the twentieth century, novels depicting the moral dilemmas and personal stresses of a generation caught up in great organizational changes with their accompanying new styles of life, tightly-designed sample surveys by behavioral scientists seeking to delineate the modal features and their consequences for the total society, sundry anthologies of the disparate impressions of recent foreign visitors to America, and proceedings of nationwide conferences assembled to evaluate one or another critical issue. It seems likely that the current decade will generate more of the same types of appraisals and appraisers.

This book is a stimulating contribution to the new literature. It is not intended as a comprehensive review of the full range of topics nor is it solely a summary of research findings. It consists, in essence, of an open-ended debate on a limited series of related issues in which the reader is invited to participate. Who might profit by an examination of these topics? What can a reader expect to learn through perusing this particular account and even vicariously joining in the discussion of the social structure of power, the role of bureaucracy in American life today, and what is meant by a democratic society?

A cross-cultural look at America provides one set of clues for answering the posed questions. Perhaps self-evident is the fact that modern American society is the object of curiosity, speculation and concern for large segments of the world — especially the new political elites and modern-oriented intellectuals of the non-Western world. Yet despite manifold efforts to convey an authentic picture of American culture, our collective research findings generally indicate scanty understanding of some of its most vital and creative aspects. To reach the selective audiences in the newly independent and sometimes neutral countries, there is need for a sophisticated account of how our social system actually functions. Attention needs to be paid to the dynamic forces reshaping our social structures, the nature of the dominant problems which confront Americans in their daily lives, the genuine dilemmas faced in attempts to relate ultimate values to specific group decisions, and the vigorous public discussions which accompany the combined attempts to assess shortcomings, achievements and future opportunities for social action. I therefore hope that copies of this book and others like it eventually find their way into the modest libraries of underdeveloped countries. In content and spirit they represent something rather important; they offer not a neat image of America but instead a clearer picture of what it means to be an American participating in an exchange of opinions concerning a basic group of public issues.

A look inside our own American academic community suggests another set of potential readers—namely, students in American colleges and universities. As an instructor in a course on modern American society, I have noticed that many students seemed baffled when asked to express their ideas on such matters as the relationship of the power-structure of a community under study with their conceptions of democratic processes, or even how they conceive the manner in which decisions are reached in a given organization. Typically one hears answers couched in formal political axioms with little regard for the social realities to which they have been exposed in a case study. There is nothing inherently wrong with the norms invoked (as, for example, the election of officers or the voting on a bond issue), but they appear far too innocent to be adopted by adults who will soon assume roles in the larger society. Perhaps by working through the cross-currents of ideas contained in this kind of book, students may undertake greater reality-testing of what they do affirm or reject.

In addition, the book offers the perceptive reader an illuminating example of a much neglected topic in that segment of the new literature which stems from the social sciences, namely, the role of the observer in relationship to what is observed. The manner of presentation should increase the capacity of the reader to make judgments about ideas which flow from research appraisals. There are important linkages to be noted while scanning any study of man and society—the observer's value commitments, the methodological style of his professional discipline, the sectors of a culture he explores, his world view. All of these influence the nature of the variables he identifies, the problems he defines as central, and the conclusions which he derives from his study of the variables and problems. Perusal of the individual treatments by these gifted scholars as they focus on a common set of phenomena will show appreciable differences in the themes they emphasize in their discussions of what constitutes power, of who has or lacks it, of the changes taking place in its distribution and so forth. The individual discussants are forthright in making explicit their separate approaches; the editors in addition skillfully analyze the areas of agreements and division. Thereafter it remains with the reader to make his independent assessments. One of the meanings of being "educated" is an awareness of how scientific knowledge is built and, perhaps more crucial, a recognition that the recipient of knowledge also has to make appraisals.

In sum, I feel the editors should be commended for bringing together not a bland series of polite statements but a stimulating discussion which raises more questions than it answers. More important, it raises questions that have to be posed in any significant appraisal of America today.

John Useem, Head of Department
Sociology and Anthropology
Michigan State University

June 12, 1961

Acknowledgments

We wish to express our indebtedness first of all to the Student Government of the University of Notre Dame. The belief of the members of this group in the importance of this topic led to their sponsorship of the Symposium out of which this book has grown. In particular, we wish to acknowledge the help and cooperation of the following members of Student Government: Andrew Lawlor, Bruce Babbitt, John Keegan, and John K. Walsh.

A special note of appreciation is extended to Dr. Benjamin Pasamanick and the Columbus Psychiatric Institute for facilitating the participation of Dr. Ehrlich in this enterprise. We are also grateful to Dr. John J. Kane, head of the Sociology Department of Notre Dame for his helpful suggestions in the planning of the Symposium and the book. Professor Donald Barrett of the Sociology Department also offered many useful suggestions. We wish to thank also Professor Warren Bilkey of Notre Dame for his critical reading of the entire manuscript. Finally, we are most appreciative of the help and guidance of Miss Emily Schossberger, Director of University of Notre Dame Press.

We are much indebted to Mrs. Deborah Luce, Carol P. Ehrlich, Mr. John Palen and especially to Mr. Charles McCollester for editing, proofing and preparing the work for the press.

Contents

Political Equality

Introduction

This book on power and democracy in America focuses on some of the key issues confronting the United States today. It is clear that political democracy as we have come to know it is being challenged by internal and external pressures that it has never before encountered. In recent years we have witnessed the prodigious growth of government not only on the federal level, but also on state and local levels. Concomitant with but to some extent preceding this growth has been the expansion of the large-scale corporate enterprise. More recently we have witnessed the phenomenal growth of labor unions, of such professional societies as the American Medical Association, and of American universities. We are just beginning to become aware of some of the consequences of this growth. We know little about how big business and big labor are or should be related to big government, or to the other big associations of American society. Are the mechanisms of our democratic system sufficiently flexible to accommodate to this new bigness? How far do the *legitimate* interests of any one institutional sector extend into another, especially into government? And conversely, how far do the interests of government extend into the other segments of American life? How are the boundaries of legitimacy defined? Finally, how can the individual maintain and protect his freedom in the face of this new—and at times overwhelming—complexity of structure? It is to questions such as these that our contributors have addressed themselves.

Professors Peter Drucker, Delbert Miller, and Robert Dahl approach this problem from very distinct vantage points, and this is clearly reflected in the content of their argument. Thus, the reader is treated to a spectrum of opposing views by a constitutional lawyer, a sociologist, and a political scientist. If there is little apparent agreement among them, there is at least a sharpening of focus on the major facets of the problem of individual freedom and decision-making in contemporary American society.

The discussion opens with a paper by Professor Drucker on "Individual Freedom and Effective Government in a Society of Super-Powers." In bold, sweeping strokes, Drucker outlines the dramatic change that has occurred in the world since 1900, the change in the power-structure and power-dynamics of society. He briefly delineates some of the major dilemmas that have arisen to face us as a result of this change—dilemmas which are worldwide in scope. The heart of his discussion is the effect of this change on the federal and local levels of government in the United States, and the consequences for the individual citizen. The following questions form the focus of his attention: (1) How to restore effectiveness to government; (2) How to prevent interest-group power-centers from usurping governmental functions; and (3) How to safeguard and strengthen the freedom of the person.

Professor Miller approaches the problem from a distinctively sociological viewpoint. His paper on "Democracy and Decision-Making in the Community Power Structure" is heavily weighted with data from his own empirical studies in this area. He is concerned basically with answering the question, what has happened to the American dream of the city beautiful and bountiful, the city as the natural center for democratic ideals and a government of limited powers.

He examines the question in terms of the most frequently alleged shortcomings of the American community: The community has lost its identity as a physical and social unity, and as a consequence has lost most of its effective leaders. Local government has become weak, community decision-making power now rests in the hands of a small circle of powerful leaders who operate outside the official governing bodies. Miller appears to concur with Drucker on some of the consequences of the transformation of the community into a metropolitan sprawl, but he and Drucker disagree on the focus of power in the contemporary metropolitan community.

Professor Dahl's paper on "Equality and Power in American Society" overlaps with both Drucker and Miller, but the overlapping produces little agreement. Dahl begins by challenging the major charges of Miller against the community, and uses his own research in New Haven to question the validity of these charges. Dahl, not unlike Drucker, perceives the community as made up of a plurality of little power-centers. He is primarily concerned with the question of the degree to which this pluralism fosters or inhibits the growth of political equality.

These papers were originally delivered in a Symposium, which featured an extended panel discussion between Professors Dahl, Drucker, and Miller. The purpose of the discussion was to attempt to clarify issues, and to ascertain the degree of difference or agreement existing among the contributors. The discussion was led by Professor Howard J. Ehrlich. It is presented here almost in its entirety. If consensus is not achieved, there is at least no doubt as to the relative positions of the principal participants. Ehrlich raises eight questions which he contends are either directly or indirectly implied in the presentations of Dahl, Drucker, and Miller. In a challenging and penetrating analysis, he proceeds to show the similarities and differences among the views of the panelists. In the ensuing discussion among Ehrlich, Dahl, Drucker and Miller, ranging over such basic issues as the conceptualization of power and the ethics of studying current political arrangements, to the more direct questions as to the kinds of power arrangements compatible with democracy and the factors determining effective government, the perspectives of our contributors are drawn in sharp relief.

The final chapter in the book has several objectives. The editors have attempted a summation of the major ideas presented in the earlier chapters. The framework of this summation is a consideration of democracy, power, and freedom and the way in which these basic concepts have entered into the formulations of Drucker, Miller, and Dahl. Secondly, we have drawn some further implications for American democracy based on this summary. These implications focus on two major classes of problems. The first class centers about the nature of our current power arrangements: the diffusion of power; the concentration of power in limited sectors of society; the concentration of power in large-scale administrative agencies; and the abdication of power by certain segments of society.

The second class of problems discussed centers about the varieties of alienation that pervade the contemporary scene—normlessness, powerlessness, and self-estrangement. Alienation, in any of its many connotations, is here viewed as inimical to participation in the democratic process.

The editors have attempted to bring forth a book which would appeal to all those who are deeply concerned about power and democracy in American society, whether they be laymen, students, or social scientists who are themselves struggling for understanding in this vast and complex area of life.

The Editors

POWER AND DEMOCRACY IN AMERICA

Peter F. Drucker, Chairman of the Management Area
of the Graduate Business School of
New York University, has written widely on
political science, economics, and business topics.
A student of public law, Professor Drucker has
contributed not only to the learned journals but to
the more popular magazines of opinion that
specialize in public affairs. Among his books are
*The New Society, The Practice of Management,
America's Next Twenty Years,* and
Landmarks of Tomorrow.

1

INDIVIDUAL FREEDOM AND EFFECTIVE GOVERNMENT IN A SOCIETY OF SUPER-POWERS

Peter F. Drucker

THE GREATEST, MOST SIGNIFICANT AND YET LEAST NOTICED OR understood of all the great changes in our century, is the change in the power-potential, power-structure and power-dynamics of society.

In 1900 when our century was born, there was but one organized power in a civilized country: the political government. In some countries it was a centralized body with local governments simply agents of the central power. In some others — the United States, Germany, Switzerland and the just emerging British Commonwealth — the system was a federal one, with local governments subordinate yet autonomous. But everywhere there was only one power-center with a complete monopoly on organized power: the "modern" government.

Yet despite its monopoly it was a strictly limited power. The Tsar of all the Russians was an "absolute monarch." Yet his secret police did not arrest Russian citizens at three in the morning; there had to be a warrant issued by proper judicial authority. Once arrested, no citizen could be kept for weeks in a police dungeon; he had to be arraigned without delay before a judge. He could not be indicted for anything but an act — opinions were not indictable. He could not be sent to Siberia without a public trial in which due process and legal rights were carefully respected. The severest punishment was life imprisonment —

there was no capital punishment, except by court martial in time of war. And in that absolutist government, decried everywhere as the blackest despotism, no one could be dismissed from government or university under suspicion of being a "loyalty risk" or a "security risk."

Outside this limited political government there were no other major powers in society. The "trusts" which frightened our grandparents so much, were, by present-day standards, about as dangerous as a pet white mouse. The worst of them all, the "octopus," Rockefeller's Standard Oil Trust, was dissolved by the Supreme Court in 1911. Every one of the dozen or so separate companies in which the court split the "monster," is today many times as big as the original parent company at its biggest. Yet only four of these descendants rank today as major oil companies. Similarly the House of Morgan that loomed like one of the Great Powers over the financial scene, never had as much capital at its disposal as is now taken in and invested every month by any one of a dozen pension trusts for the workers of a major corporation.

To be sure, there were exceptions. Our grandparents were deeply shocked, just before the turn of the century, by a scandal in France — the Dreyfus affair — which showed that the French Army was considering itself a state within the state. In Germany, across the Rhine, the Army had actually succeeded in getting its political autonomy accepted, though the informed betting around 1900 was that it would lose it again. In the late nineteenth century, for the first time in almost 300 years, the Catholic Church had emerged victorious from a struggle with a secular government that tried to subject it to its control: in Bismarck's Germany. But this, people argued, was because Bismarck, as a Protestant heading a Protestant government, had made the issue one of religion rather than one of political control. In France where Catholic in government attacked Catholic in Church, the outcome — just a few years before 1900 — had been what it had always been: a complete victory for the one power-center of what 1900 would

4

have called "modern" society, that is, the central government.

But apart from such atypical and rather rare situations, there were no particular, partial power-centers in society. There were as yet no great corporations, no nationwide labor unions, no American Medical Association, no National Education Association or similar centers. Power was centralized but strictly limited; *and society outside of government was one of diffused power, if it had any potential of power.*

Things were not very different internationally. The greater part of the world was essentially without power: all of Asia except Japan, all of Africa without exception, all of South America and Australia. There was really only one power-center in the international scene just as there was only one in the domestic scene: the Concert of Europe, the power-system of the six European "Great Powers" — Britain, France, Germany and Russia, the stars of first magnitude, and Austria-Hungary and Italy, moons rather than suns.

Again the European system was one of sharply limited power. It was organized in such a way that no one of the Great Powers was capable of defeating any two of the others. As long as only one of the Great Powers — and especially one of the "Big Four" — remained uncommitted, everybody else was therefore both safe and restrained. The system was run so as to make its maintenance the basic objective of every power's world-wide policy. The "Concert of Europe" freely disposed of large chunks of real estate all over the world — such as giving the Congo to the King of the Belgians as a private gift. Its members bickered over lines on a map, crossing an unexplored desert. They swapped populations running into the millions, and calmly carved up ancient empires into "spheres of influence." But all the deals and disputes between European powers were settled in terms of the European balance of power; every colonial issue — the conflict between Britain and France, the one between Britain and Russia, between Britain and Germany, between France and Italy — was fought out and solved as a problem of the military and power balance on the continent of Europe rather than as problems and issues of Africa or of Asia.

To be sure, in 1900 strains had begun to appear. The system was threatened by the increasing internal weakness of Austria-Hungary, which was disintegrating under the onslaught of the forces of nationalism. By 1900 it was becoming clear that there was a "Balkan problem" of great danger. No one of the Great Powers could be allowed control of the Balkans as that would have totally upset the balance. Yet the Balkan peoples themselves, the Bulgarians, Greeks, Rumanians and Serbs, seemed incapable of organizing stable nations of their own, and both, solicited and fell prey to intervention by the Great Powers.

Above all the United States and Japan, two newcomers, were already on the horizon by 1900 — though just barely. But it was not until fifteen years later, the time of World War I, that they began to rival, if not to overshadow, the old powers of Europe.

Perhaps the best indication of the international system of 1900 is the fact that there was only one country in the whole world where a white man, a European, would not be judged by men of his own color and nationality should he find himself in a court of law: Japan. And the Japanese had regained judicial sovereignty only a very few years earlier. Yet, the power of jurisdiction has everywhere and at all times been one of the fundamental attributes of independence and sovereignty.

Let us contrast this situation with our present world. Domestically, every single government has grown out of all proportion — it has become a super-power rather than the limited power of our grandparents' time. All the federal employees at the time of Theodore Roosevelt could have been housed comfortably in the smallest of the government offices in today's Washington. Our entire military establishment of that time would simply be lost on any one of our strategic air bases. Altogether, one out of every seven Americans now at work in this country of "free enterprise" and "limited government," works today for government. In 1900 it was one out of every hundred. Actually the growth has been even faster. The figures included the teachers in our public schools who were in 1900 — as they are now — the largest single employee group among government employees. They have not grown as fast as our population — the result of consolidated schools and of abolishing one-room schoolhouses. Take out the teachers and you have today one out of every four Americans in the labor force working for a government — it was one out of 500, if not one out of a thousand back in 1900.

And yet government has not grown as fast as some other nongovernmental institutions. In 1900 the social scene, in all countries, looked very much like the Kansas prairie — it was completely flat, except for one hillock, the government. The hillock wasn't high, but it loomed very large and stood all by itself. Today the social scene is very much like the Himalayas. Here are the lofty ranges of the great corporations; there the rocky cliffs of the great labor unions guarding access to job and craft; there are the great — or at least large — universities, proud of the fact that they have made a big business out of learning and that they have bigger budgets — and budget deficits — than many a fair-sized country. But there are also the many other organized powers — the farm bloc, the various professional and trade groups, to name a few. Even the churches are infinitely more organized and infinitely more powerful politically in today's America than they were in 1900.

The political government may be the Mount Everest in that landscape. But it certainly does not tower above the scene as the little hillock of a government did sixty years ago; indeed it is often hard to see it amid the mountain masses. Even more important: the political government is in danger of splitting up into separate, particular, sectional power-centers.

If, in 1900, armies defied political control, it was because of deep social and political rifts within a country. But today's armed forces may well have become uncontrollable. The army of 1900 was very much closer to Caesar's legions 1950 years earlier, than to its own grandchild, today's armed services. At the very peak of the "armaments race" before 1914, for instance, the Germans, whose military budgets frightened everybody clear out of their wits, spent a great deal less than do the Swiss today, with one tenth of Germany's population and with a long history of peace and neutrality. The Army of Imperial Germany was the greatest and most powerful military organization the world had ever seen up to that time. It was able to stand off the combined forces of Europe during World War I — and might easily have defeated them but for the United States' entry into the war. Today this army could not hold the field against the tiny but modern army of the Swiss or of the Swedes for more than a few days. But the modern army is so complex, with its size and fire power, its mobility, armor and air forces, and above all, with the dizzy speed of change in its technology, that it almost defies control. It is practically a power-center of its own, whether its own leaders want it or not.

The same goes for the bureaucracy. In 1900 Britain had the finest Civil Service, the pride of the British and the envy of every civil service reformer elsewhere. It was a Civil Service that ruled and ran the largest empire man had ever seen. But it was so small that a mere tenth of the graduates of a dozen high schools, funnelling through two undergraduate universities, were enough to staff it. It was small enough for every professional member of the Service to know all the others within two years after joining up. Today, it is impossible for the professional staff within one single agency to know each other. And the bureaucracy has become so big, so complex, so full of men of knowledge doing highly specialized work, as to be virtually uncontrollable by its nominal head, as to be virtually free from political direction.

The same thing can be said of the third major organization within government: the Foreign Service. In 1900 the Foreign Service was still pretty much what it had been when diplomacy had first become professional and organized, 250 years earlier.

8

It was still, for instance, quite common for an ambassador to write his dispatches in longhand. It was easily possible for a reasonably diligent man, like the German Kaiser, to read each dispatch personally and write — also in longhand — extensive comments on it; and there was still plenty of time left for him to do other work, let alone other things besides work.

Today's embassy is a mammoth Tower of Babel with hundreds of specialists whose purpose and mission the ambassador understands only faintly, such as specialists in agriculture and in public relations, in science and in foreign aid. And we neither know how to organize this huge activity nor how to make it an effective arm of government. It threatens, like armed service and bureaucracy, to become a power-center of its own.

Altogether, we had better realize that we have acquired a fourth, extraconstitutional branch of government: the administrative establishment, civilian and military. It is no longer, except in textbooks, an aide to the Executive but an entity of its own. To organize it for effectiveness is an urgent task. But even more urgent is the task of preventing it from becoming autonomous, from becoming a series of power-centers that are financed by government, located within government, but fundamentally powers in themselves, with their own policies, their own codes, their own self-interests.

Things are no different, by the way, in a totalitarian country. The only thing that is different is the brittle front of uniformity that hides the power struggles behind. But at the slightest weakening of the facade — at Stalin's death for instance, or in the East German, Polish and Hungarian uprisings — the organized autonomous power-centers within totalitarian society generated truly explosive forces.

Internationally we have had a parallel development. At the outbreak of World War II, the old European system was still around — though it was obviously on its last legs. But it was still possible for a Hitler to believe that by controlling and conquering Europe he could control and conquer the world. This illusion was gone by the end of World War II. But then each of two "super-powers," this country and Russia, for a short period imagined that it, and it alone, had entered into the European inheritance. These were the years when our magazines were full of talk of the "American Century." We recovered fast — it took Russia until Stalin's death (which was the reason why, until then, her foreign policy was so singularly unsuccessful except where directly supported by Russian arms). Then came a decade during which we saw the world split into two "super-powers," each with its own "bloc" of alliances and satellites.

That this was illusion, the 1960 United Nations session in New York showed clearly. What we have today is *no one power-center*. Instead, power is fragmented and atomized all over the world without any organization or any center of control.

Yet even the tiniest of these atoms, while not having enough power for constructive international activity, has, at least potentially, the power of total destruction. Nuclear armaments are not particularly difficult to make. Even the Republic of Togo — a small, underpopulated, desperately poor African state, until recently a French colony — could, within a few years, manufacture and possess enough atomic bombs to make the earth uninhabitable.

In 1900, no one in the international world had the power of destruction. And every one was safe, or could at least make himself safe. Today, by contrast, every one has, at least potentially, the power of total destruction. And no one is safe or can be made safe. Power has become atomized in the international, as it has in the domestic society. At the same time, the power-potential, so very low only sixty years ago, has increased beyond all sanity, let alone all controllability.

There are three distinct but interrelated tasks facing us as a result of this great change:

-to restore government to effectiveness both internationally and domestically;

-to prevent the new, partial, sectional or interest-group power-centers within society from usurping the functions of government and encroaching upon individual freedom and citizenship;

-to safeguard and strengthen the freedom of the person.

What we have to do, we know — at least in outline. This is not the first time in history that man has been confronted by a society dissolving into pluralism — though never before was there such doubt of his survival as there is now. Nor was the problem ever before a universal world-wide one. We know that pluralism can be a source of strength, of freedom, of achievement, if it is under Law. We know that it must lead to anarchy, and through anarchy to despotism, if it is not under Law.

What does this mean specifically — first with respect to the effectiveness of government?

I am not talking about world peace and the coming of the millenium. I am not talking of the Good Society either. I am talking about something much more modest but attainable: effective government. But unless government is first effective, is first capable of governing, of having policies and of pursuing them, all the more ambitious goals will remain mere rhetoric, promises to be mouthed by demagogues while they destroy the world.

Internationally, we need effective government the most — and can least hope to obtain it in our time of world-wide change, revolution and upheaval. But we can at least create the conditions under which leadership can be exercised and can be constructive. Obviously, this would require:

a) constant efforts to build and strengthen organs of law in international life, such as the United Nations; organs through which law can be built and can be maintained in a multinational world, in a world of conflicting ideologies, which yet is one and indivisible in this age of rapid communication and intercontinental or space missiles;

b) systematic genuine disarmament and genuine controls thereof;

c) a policy that would look upon the "neutrality" of the weaker and newer nations as a positive gain — not only for our side but for world strength and world safety. Instead of 'neutral' being considered to mean 'for the enemy,' it should be our aim to make it mean 'for our ideals and hopes.'

Our foreign policy accepted the first of these conclusions at the time of the Suez crisis. To this we owe whatever successes we have since had in international affairs. And the Soviet Union has suffered its defeats whenever it went against this first rule. With respect to the second rule, the need for disarmament and disarmament controls, neither we nor the Soviet Union have really yet fully embraced it — though the Soviet Union has had considerable propaganda advantages from its seemingly embracing it. Both countries still entertain the foolish delusion that somehow their military hegemony can be restored. In the meantime atomic contagion is spreading.

It is on the last point, the encouragement and support of genuine freedom from commitments on the part of the small and weak nations, that we in this country have failed to understand the situation and its needs. All the very real victories of communism in the last few years can be traced to the fact that the Soviets, since Stalin's death, have come to understand that genuine neutrals make possible a more effective international policy on the part of a great power, while we do not as yet understand this.

But my main interest is not in the international but in the domestic field. What do we need to make domestic government effective again — or perhaps to prevent its losing effectiveness?

One simple requirement is the focusing of the energies of government on the vital task, the task of governing — making decisions, developing policies, giving leadership and vision. That government is big today does not make it strong, any more than gross overweight makes a man healthy. It is an old rule of organization that one can either "operate" or "think." No organization — and no man by the way — can do both at the same time. Yet, the energies of modern government are absorbed by "operating."

To a large extent this is the result of our not having an effective local government. What local government we have is still based on the Greek *polis* of 2000 years ago — a small city, essentially the trading center of an agricultural area. For the new metropolis, the vast network of interlinked communities, industries, communications, power, water, sewage, transportation, that is the new "local" center of our age — whether the super-metropolis that stretches from north of Boston to Norfolk, Virginia in one disorganized sprawl, the super-metropolis that stretches from Milwaukee to South Bend and threatens to link up with Toledo and Detroit within twenty years, or the super-metropolis of Tokyo-Yokohama in Japan with its ten million people that threatens to eat up all the good farmland in a country desperately short of land — for this new power-center which is local and yet no longer within any one man's comprehension, for that we have no government. Effective national government, however, demands that local tasks be done locally; today they fall, by default, to the national government where they can only be done badly, but where also their very existence inhibits true policy, true government and national leadership.

The challenge to develop effective political theory is one of the most urgent of our time.

We can at least begin to restore effectiveness by sloughing off from government all the many activities which are obsolete, which have outlived their usefulness, which have become mere busyness. There is too much fat in government and not enough muscle, too much that provides inertia and not enough that provides energy. Sixty years ago the belief that government needed to be given more to do was justified. Today it is a sad anachronism — government needs to think more and to decide more — but to do less. Activities that no longer serve the national welfare and purpose should be ruthlessly pruned. Any modern government is overburdened with such activities — as by the way is every modern business corporation, army or labor union. Inability to eliminate is a fatal disease, in corporate bodies as well as in biological ones.

But even if government should be lean and young again, should have sweated off every ounce of fat and be in the condition of a star athlete going into the Olympic Games, the question would still remain: can government be effective with all these concentrations of sectional and interest-group power around? Can it be more than a referee between them, arbitrating between labor and management, between farmer and consumer, between Pentagon and State Department? Can it hope to accomplish more than an escape from becoming the captive of these sectional, partial powers, with the fight for control of the government degenerating into a struggle for the spoils? Lest you think this pessimistic romancing, it is already the situation with respect to those administrative agencies (such as the Federal Communications Commission which hands out radio and TV channels) which do not just "regulate" but which award rights to the public domains.

We need strong government today; we need it as we have never needed it before. We cannot get it by making government bigger — it is already too big for effectiveness. We cannot get it by destroying the sectional, particular and partial power-centers. We need those to do the daily jobs of our society. We can get effective government only if we see the role of government as that of leader, as setter of vision, as the organ of society that makes demands rather than as that which satisfies demands.

I now turn to my second question: the limits of power and authority for the new partial power-centers of society, whether they be business corporations, labor unions, medical associations or the American Association of University Professors.

By background and training — and inclination — I am a constitutional lawyer and legal historian. And the constitutional lawyer is thoroughly familiar with the problem. He has seen too many societies collapse into anarchy — and then, of course, proceed to tyranny — because partial power-centers had been allowed to usurp the functions of government. He does not have a wonder-drug for the disease. But he knows the disease and its symptoms, and at least he knows what not to do.

First the constitutional lawyer will tell you that there are three ultimate levers of control in political society. Any society that abandons those to private power groups, abandons political control. They need not be in the hands of government perhaps; at least one of the three, the control of money and credit, was, in the nineteenth century, completely decentralized. But these levers of social control must not be in the hands of partial, sectional-interest groups.

These three are:

the control of money and credit — the modern economist's way to describe the sovereign's age-old exclusive right to coin money;

the control of the dispensation of justice; and

the exclusive control over organized resistance — what the political historian used to call the right to levy armies.

Of these three, only the first one, the control of money and credit, is today largely free from control by power-groups. In respect to the dispensation of justice we see strong tendencies towards private jurisdiction — in labor relations, for instance. We are certainly right when we welcome any sign that labor and management can settle their differences — though a skeptic (and every constitutional lawyer is a skeptic) wonders where settlement ends and collusion of the two "producer interests" against the consumer and the common good begins. But we are certainly wrong, dead wrong, if we hand over to the two producer interests, management and labor — or to any others — the right to control the making of law in this area, and especially the right to administer and dispense justice.

Even more dangerous, at least by historical precedent, is the tendency — in all countries — to take whole areas of public life away from the judiciary and hand them over to administrative agencies. I am not primarily talking of regulation which applies clearly announced rules to a specific case. I am talking of the agencies — and their number is large and growing — which award and take away rights to the public domain; I have mentioned some of them earlier. Wherever in the past we had such a situation — the Court of Star Chamber of the Stuart kings is the example Americans are most likely to have heard about — it became a subverter of political authority and of the effectiveness and power of the legal sovereign. Law, all experience tells us, has to be public. Law has to be procedural; process rather than substantive law, is the citizen's safeguard and the guarantee of the law's objectivity. Law, finally, has to be law — and an administrative agency, inevitably, makes it arbitrary rather than predictable, political rather than just, dependent on influence, pressure, intimidation, if not on corruption and bribery.

And finally we are not entirely "pure" any more with respect to the third and last requirement of functioning and effective government: the absolute ban on private forces of resistance.

The power of a nationwide labor union to call out its members on strike, regardless even of national emergency, comes perilously close to the power of levying a private army. For the characteristic of an army within the body politic is not that it has rifles but that it is a disciplined, organized host, trained and capable of mass action. It serves one interest in society and is under the control and command of that interest. Any industry-wide strike comes close to that definition. (I am, let me hasten to add, a firm believer in free, decentralized — and that means nongovernmental — collective bargaining.) The industry-wide strike is no longer a strike against an employer; it is a strike against society. Whether we can permit this and maintain a functioning, effective government, I very much question.

The constitutional lawyer knows one more lesson of history. Government has been subverted as often by people assuming responsibilities that were not theirs as it has been subverted by people greedy for power. The constitutional lawyer, as I said, has a skeptical mind — at least in one respect: he suspects people who clamor for responsibility. He knows that people normally shun responsibility. And he also knows that "responsibility" is but a synonym for "authority." The one always goes with the other. He therefore suspects those who volunteer for responsibilities to be seeking power. They may act from the best of intentions and without awareness of their real aims. Nonetheless they want power to which they have no legitimate claim.

The constitutional lawyer remembers, for instance, that the destruction of government in the early Middle Ages, in the two centuries after Charlemagne, was hastened by the bishops and abbots who volunteered to take on the responsibility for the administration of justice in their estates and dioceses. These men did so with the best of intentions; in a lawless time — almost as lawless as ours — there was no justice for the poor and downtrodden against the rich, powerful and cruel. But once justice was alienated from its rightful holder, the political government, it very soon fell into the hands of the rich, powerful and cruel and became the mightiest engine for oppression.

The constitutional lawyer therefore always asks for anyone asserting responsibility: Do you have *authority* in this area? And for what and to whom will you be *accountable?* If you have no authority then you don't belong in this area — what you are after is power, not contribution. And if you are not accountable for performance to someone, you will be a despot rather than a lawful ruler.

On this basis, the constitutional lawyer and legal historian views with grave misgivings a good deal that goes on today, no matter how well-meant it may be. When business asserts its "responsibility" for "higher education," for instance, does it have any authority? I doubt it very much. Business undoubtedly has a genuine debt to education. No business in the world could run five minutes without the contribution of education. Indeed the true capital investment of a modern society is not machines but schools. I would think it eminently fair, for instance, for every business in this country to pay 1 per cent of the salary of each college graduate in its employ to the college where he graduated. This would solve the financial problem of higher education in a hurry. And if the man learned anything in college, it would be a bargain. But "responsibility of business for education" — that is a claim to a power which business has no claim to, a demand for a right for which business could not be held accountable. It is usurpation and has to be resisted.

Similarly, the constitutional lawyer would ask: what authority do labor unions have with respect to foreign policy — where they volunteer responsibility today? He would come to the same conclusion: however well-meant, however intelligent its foreign-policy proposals, the labor union, a special interest group for limited purposes of its members, who are themselves a special minority group, has no business being "responsible" for foreign policy. It has of course a right to an opinion in a free society. But that is all.

I put the "individual" first in my title — and that is where he belongs. I put him last in my paper, however; for I do not believe that one can discuss the problem of individual freedom in our society without first understanding its power-structure. It is a problem of maintaining independence even though we depend on these large, new organizations for a livelihood and for a chance to make our contribution. It is a problem of using these power-centers for the purposes of the individual rather than have the individual be used by them for theirs.

Sixty years ago the citizen in the civilized countries was working for "someone." The majority in this country, at least, worked for themselves, as a farmer, as a craftsman, as a shop- • keeper. Even though his own boss, the individual did not enjoy much real freedom of action. He was constrained by a harsh nature. He was constrained by custom. He was constrained by poverty. And of course many people, even sixty years ago, worked for someone else, worked for a "boss."

Today the great majority of people in the developed countries are employed. But they do no longer work for "someone." They work for some *organization*. Even the president of the giant corporation in which the average citizen occupies a lowly niche far down the ladder, is an employee. He can get fired — and often does. There is no one individual employer — there is the impersonal organization. It is predicated on its ability to survive the individual. The individual is transient; the organization is immortal (or thinks itself so).

And instead of the restraining forces of nature, custom and poverty, the individual, if he wants to be a person, fights against the restraints of organization. The truly dangerous ones, the • restraints that strangle the individual, are well-meaning, benevolent forces, forces working ostensibly, if not sincerely, in "the best interest of the individual."

The slavery of the inhabitants of the totalitarian countries is the result of a creed that aims at making mankind happy. The "organization man" is the creature and victim of corporate benevolence. The closing of access to jobs and skills and the freezing out of all those who are not fortunate enough to have the right credentials — a new "class system" as dangerous and as unfair as the old one ever was — is caused by work rules and union concepts "in the interest of the laboring man." The problem of • individual freedom is therefore also, in large part, a problem of guarding against well-intended concern masking a drive for illegitimate power.

For the individual to maintain himself a citizen and a person, it is first necessary that his relationship to that impersonal organization be an impersonal one, one focused on the task to be done rather than on the person. Let me say bluntly that a business corporation, a labor union, even an army or an air force, *have no business demanding loyalty from their members*. All they can demand is faithful performance of duty. Loyalty is something one earns. They also do not have any business demanding the "allegiance" of the individual. Allegiance one owes to one's God, to one's country and to one's own better self inside. One does not owe it to a temporal institution designed for very limited and partial purposes.

Finally we should realize that any attempts on the part of these institutions to cut down and to deny mobility and freedom of development and movement to the citizen, are antisocial and are actually greater threats to a free society and economy than any of the specific violations which antitrust laws try to remedy. This goes for the restrictions on access to skill, and to professions and crafts (and I include the Ph.D. requirement of our universities among these antisocial trade union restrictions). It also goes for the "golden fetters" which tie the individual to a job and to an oganization — the pension rights which he cannot take with him when he leaves; the bonuses, the compensation plan, stock options and similar fringe benefits. Designed in perfect benevolence, they are none the less threats. For the one and ultimate safeguard of freedom, as Rousseau knew almost two hundred years ago, is the freedom to emigrate, the freedom to leave and go elsewhere. And this freedom is seriously impaired today by measures taken in the interest of the individual and supposedly for his own best — but at the cost of tying him to a job, to a craft, to a skill, or at the cost of denying access to job, craft and skill to others, no matter how competent they might be.

But the individual himself has a role to play in maintaining freedom. He has first the obligation — and I use this strong word intentionally — to maintain his ability to move. In our society in which knowledge and skill change so fast, this means above all the obligation to learn how one learns.

Altogether, one ought to realize that he no longer can expect to have learned what he will need during his life when he finishes formal schooling. It used to be true that one stopped learning when he left school and began "working." Today it may be truer to say that this is the day on which one starts learning. Certainly no one can expect to do anything, fifteen years from now, for which his present learning will have adequately prepared him. The only way he can be adequately prepared is to learn how he learns.

But, in addition, the individual can stay free in this society of super-powers only if he creates his own area of personal freedom, the area outside of organized power. He must have a personal and inalienable membership in the human race and in its heritage outside and distinct from the affiliation through his organization. This of course means first the religious and spiritual life of the person. But it also means the intellectual and esthetic life. A man who plays chamber music in a string quartet twice a week, albeit as an amateur, has a sphere of freedom which no corporation, no trade union, no bureaucracy can take away from him. It is no accident that totalitarian countries are even more concerned with control of the arts than they are concerned with the control of the mind. They know the old wisdom of Plato's *Republic* — that he who controls the poetry and music of a people controls their hearts and their passions.

I am not talking of a "hobby" here. I am not talking of something that prepares a man for retirement. I am talking of an area of work, of an area of achievement, of an area of personal fulfillment. I believe that everyone today, and especially those who work for the organized power-centers around us, needs to have an independent sphere of accomplishment, something in which he is not an "employee" but his own boss, something in which he, rather than the organization, sets the goals and the standards. He need not be a master in this field — indeed none of these fields can be mastered as sidelines. But he needs to see

21

in himself more than a dilettante plying a hobby. He ought to see himself a junior journeyman. And he ought to apply to this field what my old piano teacher said many, many years ago: "You will never play Mozart like a great pianist; but there is no reason why you should not play your scales like one."

I talked about the problems which the great changes in power-structure, power-potential and power-dynamics have produced. I talked about things to watch out for. I am not altogether alarmed by the development. I view it with mixed feelings. I am conscious of the tremendous ability to achieve which our new ability to organize gives us. I am conscious of the fact that it enables us, for instance, to tackle the job of economic development. And this is not a job the aim of which is to make people rich. This is a job in which one aims to lift from mankind the age-old curse which decreed that four out of every five babies born would die before their first birthday. This is a task that aims at making man less vulnerable to the caprices of nature, and more capable to live as a man.

And I am not unconscious of — nor am I ungrateful for — the tremendous increase in our ability to advance our knowledge, advance and enrich our life through all the new horizons which our new powers open even to the ordinary man.

But I cannot say that I am altogther happy about the change. For the dangers are real — and they are great.

However, every danger is also an opportunity. And the dangers we face in this world, the dangers of a world gone power-mad, should be pre-eminently an American opportunity.

I said in the beginning that, at the turn of the century, every country had one center of power, the government. This was true even of the United States. But it was true even then that the United States had something else besides: a deep and long tradition of pluralism which refused to accept the theory on which the modern state had been based, the theory of the one absolute sovereign, the political government.

Throughout our history it has been our special concern

22

and our special ability to make the common good issue from the conflict of particular self-centered interests, and to create unity out of diversity. To this ability we owe our proudest achievements — and when, a hundred years ago, it failed us, we were plunged into our greatest national tragedy, the Civil War.

The task in the world today is to make pluralism work. Ours is and will remain a pluralist world. It is a world in which there is far too much power, especially in the international scene. But it is clear that we will be able to diminish the danger and risk of this excess of power only by making it even more pluralist than it is.

Today before the world there is one self-styled solution: the attempt to obtain uniformity by suppressing freedom, the attempt to create unity by terror. This "solution" actually does not solve anything; it only brushes the distressing evidence under the rug and, temporarily, out of sight. Whenever the terror has been lifted, if only for a week, the old forces have asserted themselves explosively. And the best proof of the total failure of this so-called solution is the steady flow of broken, wretched, desperate humanity that streams through the tiniest pin-hole in the Iron Curtain.

It is our job to find a true solution, an alternative that can organize this world of ours, with all its pluralism, with all its diversity, all its over-organization, in dignity, in peace, in hope — and in freedom. I do not say that we in this country have the answer today. I am only saying that we, of all countries, are the ones that have lived a life of pluralism, have accepted, have affirmed and made constructive a pluralist society, have believed that power should be decentralized and have lived that belief. This world of the super-power is a threat to everyone alive today, any place. But to us in this country it is also an opportunity and a challenge for leadership.

Delbert C. Miller, Professor of Sociology at
Indiana University, has largely focused his attention on
industrial and political sociology,
as the following books testify:
Industrial Sociology (with William H. Form),
Technology and Social Change (with William Ogburn.
Francis R. Allen, *et al.*),
Unternehmung, Betrieb und Umwelt (with William H. Form),
and *Industry, Labor and Community* (with William H. Form).
He has had wide experience in business and government,
having served with the Sperry-Rand Corporation,
the National War Labor Board, and the
National Wage Stabilization Agency.
He is a panel arbitrator for the
American Arbitration Association.

2

DEMOCRACY AND DECISION-MAKING IN THE COMMUNITY POWER STRUCTURE

Delbert C. Miller

DEMOCRATIC IDEALS FOR COMMUNITY LIFE

THE DEMOCRATIC WAY OF LIFE HAS ALWAYS ENCOURAGED GREAT dreams and aspirations. Perhaps this is the major reason why a dedicated democratic society has always risen to the defense of its way of life. Freedom implies not only opportunity but options — alternate ways to realize oneself.

There is a great American tradition which maintains that the local community is the *natural* center for democratic ideals. This tradition was born in the pioneer settlement and was reinforced by the American Revolution. It can be truly said we have been nourished on a basic distrust of all government. (It still takes a mighty effort to accept the policeman as our friend even when he is our next-door neighbor!) We feel most secure in a government which has only local powers. This government we can trust because we think we can control it. Moreover, we can see and hear about the results of our decisions through primary contact. Here, we have said, we can be most free. Free to live our lives with a minimum of government restraint. Free to realize our ideals with people we live with and know.

The case for individual identity with the local community is based on an intimate net of economic and social ties. Members of the community earn their livelihood within it and perhaps own their house. All of their possessions and most of their close friends are centered in the community. The quality of their children's schooling is dependent on decisions of local authority. The opportunities for leisure in parks, swimming pools, theatres, and golf courses are influenced by local facilities. Home is where the community is. The community is workshop, school, church, and social center.

In our democracy, we have pledged ourself to a noble conception of man. He is offered the right through voting to govern all matters which affect him. His channels of power begin with the freedoms of speech, assembly, and religion. They are extended through equal opportunity to information, jobs, schools, parks, homes, swimming pools, and lunch counters. They include the right to organize in unions, associations, and clubs. They encompass the right to equal representation on local policy-making boards as well as the right to run for elective office.

Some who have believed that democracy led to the progressive enrichment of all men have dreamed of cities that would nourish the life of the whole man, cities that would give high value to all the institutional activities so that the structural face of the community itself would reflect a balanced conception of the economic, political, educational, religious, welfare, and recreational activities of all the constituent members, young and old, rich and poor, white and colored.

Some have dreamed of cities of beauty incorporating aesthetic principles of form and order. There are plans in books which bring together the accumulated knowledge of architect, artist, and sociologist. These cities show careful study of land use as if the placement of buildings, streets, trees, and grass in relation to one another were of high importance. Areas are carefully delineated for buildings to serve markets, workshops, homes, churches, and recreational activities. Subcommunities are defined as sociological units in which there is built both a physical and psychological focus. Neighborhoods are constructed to serve as social units and the topography of the land is respected in the placing of streets and homes. Neighborhood services are carefully planned and located. Behind the plan is a philosophy of primary group life. It expresses itself in planning for optimum size for social interaction and for the efficient distribution of economic and social services. The individuality of a constituent community which is an ordered assembly of neighborhoods is protected by a tree belt placed around it. It contains many blind streets to break up traffic ways so that no auto driver intrudes into a community unless he has a specific purpose to accomplish there. These dreamers have talked of a society in which all men would have an opportunity to identify with groups in which they lived. Some have talked of limiting the size of cities to some optimum in which democratic participation and control could be maximized.

All of these dreams of America are possible, if Americans want them to be realized. It is an America in which the local community emerges as the center of American life. With few exceptions, there is leadership to build such pride in the efficiency and serviceability of the local community that no leviathan state need rival it in comparison. It seems feasible to entertain such an aim while endorsing the need for much state and federal power and support. It must be remembered if power can be centralized it is equally possible to decentralize power back to the local community and accompany it with richer resources. Perhaps, it is only the failure of the dreams which makes us fear this cannot be so. Certainly the dreams have been buffeted by the impact of social trends. In fact, for some, the community aspirations have never arisen, and for others, the aspirations seem impossible of attainment. They have already written off the local community as an obsolete unit lacking any meaningful relation to the large decisions of war and peace, economic progress, and social development. Let us see why this is so.

INDICTMENTS OF THE COMMUNITY AS A SOCIOLOGICAL UNIT

There are five major indictments of the local community

which charge it with failure to function as an effective political and social unit. These are:

1) It has lost its social solidarity.

2) It has lost its identity as a physical reality.

3) It has lost most of its effective leaders.

4) Its political institutions are weak.

5) The power over community decisions rests with a small, inner circle of power leaders who operate outside of official governing bodies. Fear, pessimism, and silence dominate the community social climate.

Each of these is a serious charge. Each will therefore be carefully examined.

LOSS OF SOCIAL SOLIDARITY

The disrupting effects of industrialization can be observed very early in the evolution of an agrarian society to an industrial society. Emile Durkheim's writing at the turn of the twentieth century explained that these social disruptions were caused by the increased division of labor which accompanied industrialization.[1] He said that societies are not mere aggregates of people, they are shared ways of life characterized by social solidarity. Whereas the social solidarity of mankind in the past was based on such things as kinship, friendship, and such, in the modern world social solidarity is increasingly based on a division of labor. This creates an increased dependence of modern man on his fellow man. Yet the division of labor often creates the negation of solidarity. Occupational divisions stimulate the forming of splinter groups, causing class disturbances, labor struggles, and various social and industrial crises. This comes about because the sources of all such difficulties are in the collective sentiments—rules, regulations, and norms—which are the essence of society

[1] Emile Durkheim, *The Division of Labor in Society,* translated by George Simpson (Glencoe, Illinois: The Free Press, 1947).

and social solidarity. Division of labor prevents the rise of appropriate norms, and anomie or normlessness prevails. Thus, in the midst of high functional interdependences man's social life becomes more segmented in both its economic and noneconomic spheres. Karl Polanyi in *The Great Transformation* accepts this interpretation and says that the emerging market economy dissolved society.[2] It broke up the family and made people spiritually homeless. It pulled them off their farms and their crafts and herded them into the city and into the factories. It offered a mechanical institution revolving around money prices for the organic human institutions which mankind had always known. For thousands of years, markets had been dependent on society; men came first, money, second. The nineteenth century reversed this process and linked all local societies in a vast, international market. Control over the local economy was irretrievably lost and men everywhere became dependent on economic and social repercussions emanating from distant parts. Tensions explode in disorders, wars, and revolutions. The individual in our cities has learned to put down shallow roots and keep his baggage light. William H. Whyte in *The Organization Man* describes the middle management community, Park Forest, Illinois, as a stopover community for modern career men whom he calls "transients"[3] — and with good reason. In Park Forest about 35 per cent of the population turned over annually.

Charles H. Cooley at Michigan also saw these changes and at the turn of the twentieth century wrote of the changes occurring in social participation. He noted that small primary group-life is being replaced by the larger secondary group. Impersonal and formalized contacts, varied but shallow, are replacing the personal and many-sided group-life of an agrarian

[2] Karl Polanyi, *The Great Transformation* (New York: Farrar and Rinehart, 1944).

[3] William H. Whyte, Jr., *The Organization Man,* (New York: Simon and Schuster, 1956).

society.[4] And Lewis Mumford said that our cities are emerging into a megalopolis stage where human and social values are being lost under the massive swirls of large populations and the ever greater subordination of life to the machines and to the threat of war.[5]

W. Lloyd Warner and J. O. Low reconstructed some of these changes by studying a shoemaking plant in a small 300-year-old New England industrial town.[6] In the course of the nineteenth century the economic life of Yankee City came to be dominated by one industry—shoemaking. Shoemaking changed from a hand craft based on the family to mass production. The job was "deskilled." Ownership of materials, tools, and products passed from the family to local owner-managers and finally to people living outside of Yankee City. The market for shoes became widened to include the nation, then the world.

Two changes were selected for more detailed examination: the worker's status in the factory and the community, and the participation of factory owners and managers in the life of Yankee City. Mass production eliminated the skill hierarchy in which the young had learned from their elders ways of life as well as their craft, and in which they had found that integrity of existence which is called "security." Age-grade status was destroyed and job security could no longer be found in the skill of the workman: only a union appeared to be a defense against the brutal consequences of industrialization.

As long as the factories were owned and managed by residents of Yankee City, they were in many ways subject to local control. The owners, managers, and financiers were recognized leaders in the community and participated in all its affairs. These men were imbued with local sentiments which moved them, for

[4] Charles H. Cooley, *Social Organization* (New York: Charles Scribners, 1900).

[5] Lewis Mumford, *The Culture of Cities* (New York: Harcourt, Brace, 1938), pp. 223-99.

[6] W. Lloyd Warner and J. O. Low, *The Social System of the Modern Factory* (New Haven: Yale University Press, 1947).

instance, "to take care of their own people." With the transfer of ownership to "outsiders," living elsewhere, most of these local ties snapped. The workers lost contact with their employers. People in the highest social positions in the community were isolated from the community's main industry. Then in the depths of the Great Depression of the 1930's the shoe workers of Yankee City, to the very last man, went out on strike—a completely unprecedented and unexpected happening. Thus did the market economy burst upon Yankee City as it has upon so many other American communities. Social solidarity was weakened as anomie became more prevalent. This is coupled with a second indictment.

Loss of Physical Identity

The community has generally connoted people living in one locality or region under the same culture and having some common geographical focus for their major activities. Such a community had recognizable boundaries which delineated activities inside and bounded them at the perimeter where rural life began. Today the average community may be marked by sprawl within and vast layers of suburbanization and rural-urban fringes outside. All of this is tied into such great networks of rapid communication and transportation that the community emerges more like a node in a vast world market. Graham Wallas in *The Great Society* writes of one industrial community:

> The whole of Bromstead . . . is a dull, useless boiling-up of human activities, an immense cluttering of futilities. . . . It is as unfinished as ever; the builders' roads still run out and end in mid-field in their old fashion; the various enterprises jumble in the same hopeless contradiction—if anything intensified. Pretentious villas jostle slums, and sculleries gape towards the railway, their yards hung with tattered washing unashamed; and there seem to be more billboards by the railway every time I pass, advertising pills and pickles, tonics and condiments, and such like solicitudes of a people

31

with no natural health or appetite left in them.[7]

Sprawl is more than an aesthetic problem. It indicates that the individuality of constituent neighborhoods and subcommunities has been weakened or destroyed. And at the boundaries of the central city a new phenomenon may be observed. There is no rural landscape. In its stead appear vast clumps of suburbs, satellite cities, crossroad markets, factories, and rural-urban fringe developments.[8] During the last twenty years, the growth of population has been much more rapid outside of the central city than within. In Suburbia live one third of the nation, roughly 60 million people, who represent every patch of democracy's handstitched quilt, every economic layer, every laboring and professional pursuit in the country. No wonder it has been written that Suburbia in the 1960's is the grass roots of the United States. It is, as Max Lerner has put it, "the focus of most of the forces that are remaking American life today." Humorist-Exurbanite James Thurber has observed the steady spread of Suburbia and says, "this country will be called the United Cities of America, one suburb will pile into another until in New York State there'll only be Albany and New York City; and they can really fight it out in the streets. If they start shoveling in San Diego, buildings will tumble in Bangor." This movement to Suburbia has repercussions on urban leadership and leads to the third indictment.

Loss of Devoted Leadership

What Suburbia gains, the city often loses. A highly qualified potential community leader who rushes from his office or plant to catch the 5:30 train for Westchester, Silver Springs, or Park Forest is not likely to come back to the central city for an evening meeting of some voluntary group. His new allegiance is trans-

[7] Graham Wallas, *The Great Society* (New York: Macmillan, 1917), pp. 6-7.
[8] *The Suburban Community,* edited by William Dobriner (New York: G. P. Putnam's Sons, 1958).

ferred or at least split as the suburban home community claims his attention. Research shows that those Top Influentials who have remained active in the central city are moving increasingly to the suburbs. Spot maps show an almost complete exodus for business and professional leaders. Only two exceptions may be noted. Labor leaders and ministers seem to maintain residences in the central city. Labor leaders remain because they are often of lower income status and perhaps believe they should live close to their industrial constituents. Ministers often occupy parish houses provided by the church. But for these two exceptions the daily march is back to the ranch house in the hills, with week-end retreats away from the workshop that is the city. It is alleged that suburbanites live like parasites on the city, taking away from it wealth and services but giving back to it less and less in the way of support and leadership. Leaders used to live in the city and breathe its very problems. Now riding in their autos, taxis, buses, and trains, they glide in and out like men in a culture bubble protected from the sprawling industrial landscape and its problems.

It is the problems of the suburban community and problems down at the office of city workshops which engage them. But problems of the larger city fall into the only hands left to deal with them. This trend is further complicated by other developments. The growth of the corporation with its absentee ownership has brought the salaried manager into business control and prestige. For this he has been asked by many corporate directors to pay a price by conforming to a prescribed community role.

Pellegrin and Coates have shown that absentee-owned corporations play a vital role in civic affairs within Bigtown, a Southern city of approximately 200,000.[9] This city has had a meteoric growth based on the new industrial plants which were built by absentee-owned corporations. Community projects are

[9]   Roland J. Pellegrin and Charles H. Coates, "Absentee-Owned Corporations and Community Power Structure," *American Journal of Sociology,* March, 1956, pp. 413-19.

usually doomed if they lack the approval of these new corporations. Top executives communicate with one another informally and arrive at agreement on matters of policy. The executives of each corporation are then informed of the decision, making it possible for given community projects to be supported or vetoed by united action.

Typically, the absentee-owned corporation has a list of executives eligible for membership in power-wielding civic organizations. Community leaders expect the corporations to provide civic leadership commensurate with their size, and the corporation expects adequate representation in all groups which chart the course of community affairs. Executives are expected to serve in selected civic posts as part of their job. An executive gets a clearance from his superior permitting him to serve. The researchers report that one interviewee told them:

> Only a man who is naive would accept invitations to participate in important community affairs without the blessings of Mr. A., the top executive of our company. For a man to ignore the usual procedure for getting clearance, he'd either have to be unconcerned about his career or be a complete ass. In fact, in my company, executives at any level have to clear all their organizational memberships with top management.[10]

It has been pointed out that the executive depends for his career advancement upon his superiors rather than upon local individuals or institutions, and hence he is much more concerned with the affairs of the corporation than he is with those of the community.

Pellegrin and Coates affirm this to be true of the absentee-owned corporation executives in Bigtown but list other motives for civic activity such as altruism, desire for power and feeling of respect gained in community participation, and a sense of personal independence not possible inside the corporation.

[10]   *Ibid.*, p. 417.

Another researcher in a small midwestern industrial community of some 20,000 inhabitants has reported that there has been a withdrawal of the most important economic leaders from participation in community affairs.[11] He believes this to be related to three social factors: (*a*) the establishment by a growing number of locally-owned industrial units of direct supplier relationships with a small number of large, non-local manufacturing plants; (*b*) the subsequent introduction into the local economic system of an increasing number of branch plants of large, absentee corporations; and (*c*) the concomitant dissolution of the extensive networks of interlocking directorates and officerships which had formerly served to link significant numbers of local economic dominants within the community. As the top economic leaders, and especially those representing the growing number of large, absentee-owned corporations, have withdrawn from community affairs, the overt direction of the political and civic life of the community has passed almost wholly into the hands of a group of middle-class business and professional men, almost none of whom occupies a position of economic dominance. The absentee-owned corporations are taking a "hands off" position with regard to local political decision making. The corporations are interested in "making friends" but "getting involved" is regarded as inconsonant. Meaningful participation in the decision-making processes of a community is mainly regarded as entailing risks of alienation to their operation and to their positions in the larger social system—risks which could not be offset by any palpable advantages through playing significant roles in the local power structure.

A study of an Ohio town has corroborated a number of these trends. Rossi reports that the absentee manager appears to be motivated to participate in local affairs mainly through corporation pressures; his role, however, is defined as "get involved but

[11] Robert O. Schulze, "The Role of Economic Dominants in Community Power Structure," *American Sociological Review,* February, 1958, pp. 3-9.

at no risk to the company."[12] Above all, the executive is not supposed to lose—"losing" being defined as arousing or becoming enmeshed in controversy. The pressures, therefore, induce managers toward "safe" activities which demonstrate corporate and individual good fellowship. *Participation is required, but not leadership.* Local leaders and politicians are placed in an anomalous position. Most of them are aware of the lack of real interest on the part of the absentee executives and are frustrated in their attempts to get them involved. On the other hand, local politicians with outside connections are in a position to cause embarrassment and trouble for absentee corporation managers. This merely adds up to yet another reason why the latter executives avoid community involvement.

TOLERANCE OF WEAK POLITICAL INSTITUTIONS

Peter Rossi says, "a separation between local government and the local elites of wealth, intellect and status has become firmly entrenched on the local scene. The local echelons of the party organizations and the elective offices of municipal, county and even state governments are manned by persons whose social positions are often many levels below the denizens of the Country Club, Rotary Club and the Chamber of Commerce. The city fathers and the county commissioners are recruited, at best, from among local lawyers of somewhat uncertain income and miscellaneous clientele, and more likely from among small proprietors and professional politicians. Money, status and intellect seem in one place and political control in another. Such anomalies lead to the hypothesis that things are really not what they seem and that somewhere there are strings which exist by means of which local government is guided from without.

"How things 'get done' has therefore become more and more problematical as the lack of articulation grows between the

[12] Peter H. Rossi, "Report to Harvard Community Power Structure Conference," Cambridge, Mass., April 26-27, 1958.

36

political elite and the industrial, commercial, and professional elites, Rossi finds it hard to believe that a corner grocer elected mayor can govern independently in a modern industrial community. He may have authority, but how can he withstand the influence of local business elite? Rossi perceives "a seeming mushiness to the decision-making process on the local scene, an ambiguity of structure which is hard to tolerate. So much appears on the surface to be haphazard, idiosyncratic, and unique that it is both hard to believe and hard to study."[13]

POWER-CENTERS OUTSIDE GOVERNMENT

Floyd Hunter reports on his study of Regional City that there is a power hierarchy and at the top a group of policy-makers. "These men are drawn largely from the businessmen's class. They form cliques or crowds, as the term is more often used in the community, which formulate policy."[14]

He then generalizes to say, "fear, pessimism, and silence are three elements in the behavior of individuals with which any community organizer, or social analyst, must deal. . . . Expressions of fear in community life are prevalent among the top leaders. Pessimism is manifested among the professionals, and silence is found in the mass of the citizenry in Regional City."[15] He explains that fear is manifest in a cautious approach to any new issue which may arise and is apparently rooted in the feeling that any change in the existing relations of power and decision in the community would be disastrous for those who now hold power. Even opening of channels of communication is frowned upon by control leaders lest undesirable elements may be brought into the policy-making situation. The fear is strongly experienced in reference to the growing power of the Negro group. A kind of

---

[13] Peter H. Rossi, "The Study of Decision-Making in the Local Community," Mimeo, University of Chicago, August, 1957. pp. 4-5.
[14] Floyd Hunter, *Community Power Structure* (Chapel Hill: University of North Carolina Press, 1953), p. 113.
[15] *Ibid.,* p. 228.

"trickle-down" theory of power is applied by relying on dominant figures to sanction policy.

The professional workers in the planning and social agencies are especially susceptible to moods of pessimism. They are employed by and subordinated to the upper structure of power whose interests they are supposed to represent, yet in most cases they work with underprivileged persons. To make the needs of their clients known is difficult. The professional is isolated from the upper reaches of power and he feels that no professional person may be critical of many power decisions without incurring an attack damaging to his career in the community.

The bulk of the population in Regional City is silent because there is almost no way to have a voice in policy making outside of their right to vote for city officials. But important policy is made outside of the official governing bodies. To have a significant voice one must reach the unofficial power-structure. Participation in many of the organizations in Regional City would merely give the individual a social experience of being with his fellows. Many groups are not "political" in nature and have no influence in community decision-making. Many groups exist to maintain the status quo. The road into the power-structure is open but is hedged with numerous barriers.

These five indictments have been presented for evaluation. If they are proved true or even partially so, democratic functioning in the local community must be accepted as an unfinished business of serious gravity. We must now turn to the available knowledge of community power-structures.

THE COMMUNITY POWER-STRUCTURE

The community power-structure refers to the Key Influentials, the Top Influentials, the community power-complex, and all those parts of the institutionalized power-structure of the community which come into play when activated by a community concern.[16]

16 William H. Form and Delbert C. Miller, *Industry, Labor, and Community* (New York: Harpers, 1960), pp. 437-48.

COMPONENTS OF COMMUNITY POWER-STRUCTURE

In order to appreciate the full range of community power, five of its components must be taken into account. Each of these components will be first briefly defined and later elaborated.

1) The *institutionalized power-structure of the society* refers to the relative distribution of power among societal institutions.

2) The *institutionalized power-structure of the community* refers to the relative distribution of power among local institutions.

3) The *community power-complex* is composed of permanent or temporary organizations, special interest associations, and informal groups which act in matters of general community concern and which are *not normally handled* by the functioning of local institutions.

4) The term *top influentials* refers to a number of influential persons from whom particular decision-makers are drawn into various systems of power relations according to the community issues or projects that arise.

5) The term *key influentials* refers to the acknowledged sociometric leaders among the top influentials in given issues.

These components, as diagrammed in Figure 1, range from general diffuse conditioning sources of control to concrete forces exerted in specific community issues.

Each component beginning with the first may be thought of as successively conditioning the following component. However, the five components must not be thought of as a single integrated social structure, but rather as a number of interpenetrating categories which can sensitize the observer to the wide sources of influence exerted generally and specifically.

Key Influentials

$+$

Top Influentials

$+$

Community Power
Complex

$+$

Institutionalized Power-Structure of the Community

$+$

Institutionalized Power-Structure of Society

Figure 1. *The five components of Community Power-Structure.*

Institutionalized Power-Structure of Society

Properly speaking the Institutionalized Power-Structure of Society is not a community component of power. Yet it is necessary to refer to it because all communities are tied into the broader society. In the long run there is a strain for local institutional relations to approximate those of the broader society. In American society the national power of business, labor, and government provides a distinctive umbrella of power over local communities.

Institutionalized Power-Structure of the Community

The Institutionalized Power-Structure of the Community is a relatively permanent distribution of institutional power which directly conditions the exercise of community power.

The Institutionalized Power-Structure of the Community must not be thought of as a crude ranking of the power held by each institution, because each institution in a sense has most power in its particular arena, and because reciprocal rather than hierarchical relations characterize institutional life. Rather the Institutionalized Power-Structure of the Community should be thought of as a latent pattern of power relations which reflects the relative importance of the values attached to institutional functions in the society, the relative material resources of the institutions, the relative effectiveness of their sanctions, and their relative ability to initiate societal changes.

There may be local variations where educators dominate business, local government, newspaper policy, education, welfare and even religion. This may be the case in small communities where the university is the largest employer. In other communities, religion may occupy a relatively more dominant role. Such appears to be the case in Rimrock, New Mexico. Vogt and O'Dea compared this community with Homestead, Texas. Both communities differed primarily because of the importance of the Mormon Church in Rimrock. Rimrock's original development was possible because a water association was informally developed around and within the church. After World War II returning veterans had to choose between underemployment or leaving the community. Land was bought for the veterans through funds borrowed from the Church Welfare Plan Agency. In another situation, the villagers, acting through the church organization, decided to have the town's streets gravelled. The plan to build a high-school gymnasium was discussed in a Sunday priesthood meeting at the church. Arrangements were made for each able-bodied man to contribute 50 hours of labor or $50 for construction. Weekly dances are held as part of the general church recreation program of the community.

Obviously, domination of community institutions by the church or another institution is almost impossible in larger cities in the U.S. However, the domination of the economic institution may be blunted by the presence of large groups whose values are strongly expressed by noneconomic institutions such as government, education, welfare, or religion. One way in which the relative dominance of institutions is reflected is in the number of institutional elite representatives which arise in community organizations.

Community Power-Complex

The Community Power-Complex refers to a power arrangement among the temporary or permanent organizations, special-interest associations, and informal groups emerging when they act in specific projects or issues. These projects and issues are usually those not handled by the functioning of local institutions. In the day-to-day functioning of the community many groups want to sponsor certain community projects. Some succeed with no apparent opposition. Most of the attempts do not gain community acceptance because not enough interest develops for them, or because they are quietly vetoed by a powerful organization, or because they are absorbed as a project by a specific association. Occasionally, however, groups succeed in establishing their projects, despite furious resistance by other groups. The continuous process of sponsoring projects, developing issues, gaining support, and marshalling opposition for local projects and issues has relevance for the distribution of community power.

The Community Power-Complex, unlike the Institutionalized Power-Structure of the Community, is issue-relevant in an action context. It is an emergent organization which arises out of the interaction of concrete organizations in specific situations. It represents a major source of fluidity in the community power-structure. In specific projects or issues the power-arrangements among the organizations may deviate considerably from that of the Institutionalized Power-Structure of the Community, especially for low-level issues or projects. In high-level issues involving the entire community, the internal power-arrangement of the Community Power-Complex tends to approximate that of the Institutionalized Power-Structure of the Community.

The factors preventing a simple transformation of the Institutionalized Power-Structure of the Community into the

Community Power-Complex in concrete issues are many. In the first place, specific issues may not involve the interests of many associations in several of the local institutions. Secondly, although an issue may affect the interest of an organization its leaders may be unaware of it, or if aware, not moved to act. More important, many organizations such as the Chamber of Commerce, Parent-Teacher Association, and American Legion, are internally very heterogeneous, so that their members may be split on whether the organization should enter into a fray and what positions it should take. Fourth, people play multiple roles, so that several organizations to which they belong might take contrary positions on a single local issue. For these and other reasons, it is best to view the Community Power-Complex as a field of forces which will be resolved in a given direction, once the participants and their characteristics are known.

Top Influentials

The term Top Influentials refers to a number of influential persons from whom particular decision-makers are drawn into various systems of power-relations according to the community issues and projects that arise. Often, the Top Influentials are also heads of business firms, labor unions, institutional elite representatives, and officials of powerful associations in the Community Power-Complex. However, people in such positions, high "society" leaders and other leaders are not necessarily in the Top Influential pool. Rather, the Top Influentials are composed of influential persons who have been actively interested and involved in community issues and projects in the past. As will be demonstrated later, they do not necessarily form an integrated social system, but rather potential decision-makers or project leaders, who have demonstrated by their past activities a concern for community problems, the ability to initiate organization in community affairs and the capacity to influence the direction of policy of the associations to which they belong and the policies of community-wide organizations. They also have the power to veto a threatening action on the part of others.

The Key Influentials

The Key Influentials are significant because they are the acknowledged leaders of the Top Influentials. As such they exercise great influence either in initiating or sanctioning a project or issue. Veto power can be especially significant in their hands. Research has indicated that a "no" from a Key Influential could often stop a project before it got started.

Two questions seem especially crucial to ask about the community power-structures in our communities: Do businessmen dominate community power-structures in American communities? Do key influentials influence policy-making by acting in concert through cliques?

My own research has been directed at these questions and I should like to report the findings. Floyd Hunter reports from his Regional City study that businessmen do dominate policy-making by utilizing a closed-clique structure in which each clique has a leader. The question arises as to the prevalence of this form of domination. To make one test I fashioned a research design which would compare two cities with Regional City.[17] I selected a city in the Pacific Northwest and one in the Southwest of England. Each city, Regional, Pacific, and English, has a similar population of about 400,000; they have similar economies and possess many common social and cultural features. I followed closely the research methods of Floyd Hunter to insure close comparability of results obtained. I sought an answer to the question, "Do businessmen dominate community decision-making?" The following steps in the method were taken:

1) Lists of leaders were secured from organizations and informants in nine institutional sectors: (*a*) business and finance, (*b*) education, (*c*) religion, (*d*) society and wealth, (*e*) political

[17] *Ibid.*, pp. 589-97.

and governmental organization, (*f*) labor, (*g*) independent professions, (*h*) cultural (aesthetic) institutions, and (*i*) social service. The initial lists included a total of 312 names in Pacific City and 278 in English City.

2) Ten expert panel raters were selected on the basis of the following qualifications: (*a*) knowledge of the leaders in one institutional sector with special thoroughness, (*b*) broad knowledge of the community, (*c*) many contacts with Top Influentials but not themselves Key Influentials. Raters meeting these qualifications are commonly found among public relations officials, newspaper reporters, and some government officials. Raters were asked to designate each person as most influential, influential, or less influential on the specific criterion: "Person participates actively either in supporting or initiating policy decisions which have the most effect on the community." Those nominated most frequently as most influential were selected for interviewing.

3) Personal interviews were held with a 50 per cent stratified random sample of 44 Top Influentials in Pacific City and 32 Top Influentials in English City. The sample had been stratified according to the nine institutional sectors enumerated above, and corresponding proportions of leaders from each sector were interviewed. During the interview each Top Influential was asked the following question: "If you were responsible for a major project which was before the community that required decision by a group of leaders—leaders that nearly everyone would accept—which ten on this list would you choose, regardless of whether they are known personally to you or not? Add other names if you wish."

4) Each respondent was asked to check a social acquaintance scale for each Top Influential by *don't know, heard of, know slightly, know well, know socially* (exchange home visits). He was also asked to check each Top Influential with whom he had worked on committees during the past two years.

5) The interview included questions on current issues, role

played by respondent, persons and organizations that worked for and against issues. Ratings were also secured of influential organizations and associations in the community. The interview concluded with the question: "There are several crowds in (Pacific City) that work together and pretty much make the big decisions. Is this true or false?" The responses were probed.

The results may be observed in Table 1. Table 1 shows the institutional affiliation of the Top Influentials selected by the panels in the three cities. Business has the largest representation among the Top Influentials but there is a considerable spread over the other institutional sectors. A *chi square* test applied to the frequency distribution in the three cities failed to reveal any significant variation in the panel selections. However, a different pattern emerged when the Key Influentials were selected by the Top Influentials themselves.

Table 1. *Top Influentials By Institutional Affiliation As Selected By Expert Citizen Panels*

Institutional Affiliation	Pacific City (N=44) Per cent	English City (N=32) Per cent	Regional City (N=40) Per cent
Business	33	34	58
Labor	14	19	5
Education	10	9	5
Government	17	9	5
Independent professions*	12	13	15
Religion	7	9	0
Society and wealth	0	7	12
Social welfare and cultural leaders (combined)	7	0	0
Total	100	100	100

* Hunter says that both of the lawyers in Regional City are corporation lawyers. I have been inclined to classify them as part of the business representation, but I have not because they are lawyers of independent law firms. Lawyers are classified under independent professions unless they were reported as salaried employees in a business firm.

The Key Influentials are a significant feature of any community power-structure for they are the sociometric leaders. The initiation and sanction of policy tends to be centered about them so that they may greatly influence the values which dominate in decision-making. The Key Influentials are those persons who were most often chosen by the Top Influentials as the leaders they would want if they were responsible for a major project before the community and they were seeking leaders nearly everyone would accept.

The twelve influentials with the highest sociometric choice status for the three cities are shown in Table 2.

In Pacific City and Regional City of the United States, business representation predominates among the Key Influentials. A comparison of the proportions of business representation within the Top Influentials (Table 1) and the business representation within the Key Influentials (Table 2) reveals that the Top Influentials chose businessmen more frequently as Key Influentials, in the two American cities. In contrast, English City retains a representation of business among its Key Influentials (25 per cent) that corresponds closely to the business representation among its Top Influentials (34 per cent). Moreover, English City reveals a more even representation from the various institutional sectors of the community among its Key Influentials.

This marked difference between the American cities and English City raises questions about community organization. Why should two labor leaders be among the outstanding leaders in English City while not one labor leader appears among the Key Influentials of the two American cities? These and other questions will be explored later when the findings of further analysis have been presented.

Evidence for the influence of the Key Influentials was sought by establishing measures of actual behavior for all the Top Influentials. These measures included the activity of Top Influentials in committee work as reported in the newspapers over a two-year period, and by their own statements of committee

Table 2. *Key Influentials As Selected By Top Influentials And Ranked By Status As Influential Policy Makers*

Pacific City	*English City*	*Regional City*
Manufacturing executive	Labor party leader	Utilities executive
Wholesale owner and investor	University president	Transport executive
Mercantile executive	Manufacturing executive	Lawyer
Real estate owner—executive	Bishop, Church of England	Mayor
Business executive (woman)	Manufacturing executive	Manufacturing executive
College president	Citizen party leader	Utilities executive
Investment executive	University official	Manufacturer owner
Investment executive	Manufacturer owner	Mercantile executive
Bank executive—investor	Labor leader	Investment executive
Episcopalian bishop	Civic leader (woman)	Lawyer
Mayor (lawyer)	Lawyer	Mercantile executive
Lawyer	Society leader	Mercantile owner
Business representation: 67 per cent	Business representation: 25 per cent	Business representation: 75 per cent

participation. Likewise, we sought evidence of their activity as spokesmen in community life as reported by the newspapers. Participation scores were derived from adapted Chapin Social Participation scales for social, civic, professional, and other business affiliations.

Table 3 shows the Spearman rank-order correlations of the Top Influentials for these various forms of community behavior in Pacific City and English City.

Table 3. *Spearman Rank-Order Correlations Derived from Policy Committee Choice Rankings of Top Influentials and Ranking on Various Measures of Community Behavior*

Policy Committee Choice Rank Compared With:	Pacific City (N=44)	English City (N=32)
Committee appointments accepted during past two years, as shown by newspaper reports	.51	.43
Committee participation for two year period, as designated by Top Influentials on the interview schedule	.84	.67
Newspaper mentions of community activities and statements	.15	—.31
Participation in other businesses as owner or director	.53	.33
Participation in social clubs	.51	.47
Participation in civic-organizations	.58	.43
Participation in professional organizations	.45	.34
Total social participation in business, social, civic, and professional organizations	.59	.48

These correlations indicate that there is a definite correspondence between the policy committee choices designating Key Influentials and actual behavior patterns in both Pacific City and English City. The highest correlation is shown to be that between policy committee choice rank and the committee participation for a two-year period as designated by the Top Influentials on the interview schedule.

Conclusion

Validity of the Key Influentials as identified is now assumed to be demonstrated with sufficient confidence to validate the hypothesis for Pacific City. Businessmen do exert a predominant influence in community decision-making in Pacific City and Regional City. Indeed, this statement may now be generalized.

Recent findings from a large research project based on studies of community power-structures in a group of Southwestern (U.S.) and Mexican cities have been reported by Charles P. Loomis and his associates. These findings make substantial confirmation of the domination of businessmen in community decision-making. The occupations of Key Influentials have been identified for El Paso, Denver, Tucson, Las Cruces, San Diego, McAllen, Cd. Juarez, and Tijuana. Comparisons with Pacific City, English City, and Southern City show the following results:

Sixty-three per cent of the Top Influentials were from business. Ten out of the eleven cities reported at least one financier among the Key Influentials with a total of 30 (almost a quarter) being named in all. Only English City and Las Cruces failed to produce a financier in the top group. Both of the relatively specialized categories of manufacturing and merchandising were represented in at least eight cities. The merchants, including both wholesale and retail, produced slightly over one fifth of the Key Influentials, with English City and El Paso failing to contribute to this category. Among manufacturers who were almost a sixth of all Key Influentials, only Tucson and Las Cruces were not represented. This may be explainable by the relative absence of manufacturing in the economic base of these cities.

The most frequently chosen occupational category outside of business was that of the lawyer, represented eight times in seven cities. It may be that the lawyer is becoming an effective link between business and other sectors of the community.

Mayors were chosen as Key Influentials in five of the ten cities, while other governmental officials and political leaders were chosen nine times in four cities. While it may be argued that the hierarchical structure of local government makes it likely that the mayor will be most often chosen from among governmental officials, the fact that mayors were not chosen as Key Influentials in five of the cities suggests the need for further exploration of the place of government in the community power-structure.

Labor is notably lacking representation in the influence structure in all communities except English City. In like manner, agriculture is represented only in Las Cruces by two of the 13 persons listed; one of the two is at the very top of the list. Religion, education, society and wealth, welfare, social and cultural leaders have only scattered representation.

However, in English City, the Key Influentials come from a broad representation of the institutional sectors of community life. Why should this difference exist between the American cities and the English city? Two major factors seem to explain much of this difference. The first is the difference in occupational prestige values between the United States and England. In contrast to the United States "the social status of industry in England and so of its captains, is low by comparison with the law, medicine, and the universities." Top business managers are recruited from the universities (and upper-class families) where the tradition of a liberal education predominates, and this kind of education emphasizes humanistic values and minimizes the business orientation that characterizes the social climate of the typical American university campus. Many top business leaders, educated at Oxford and Cambridge, reported during interviews that they regarded business life as a very useful activity but did not view it as occupying the whole man. They expressed a respect for scholarly pursuits. Indeed, specialized courses in business administration in the university are very few, and the tradition continues that business management is learned by experience within the firm. This value system plays a role in the selection of community leaders in English City just as the larger emphasis and prestige of business leadership influences the selection of community leaders in the two American cities.

A second major factor is the structure of city government. In Pacific City the city council is composed of nine members elected at large on a nonpartisan ballot. These nine members have the following occupational affiliations:

Newspaper owner-editor (District Paper)	Business
Merchant	Business
Merchant	Business
Newspaper owner-editor (District Paper)	Business
Merchant	Business
Merchant	Business
Housewife (formerly teacher)	Professional
Jeweler (and labor officer)	Skilled worker
Bus operator	Semi-skilled worker

A background of small business predominates. None of the council members was chosen as a Top Influential by our panel raters or by Top Influentials. There is every indication that the top community leaders do not regard the council as a strong center of community power. The council tends to make decisions on community issues after a relatively long period of debate and after power mobilization has taken place in the community. During this period such groups as the Chamber of Commerce, the Labor Council, Municipal League, Parent-Teachers Association, and Council of Churches take stands. Council members may be approached and appeals made to them. Newspaper editors write articles. Key Influentials may make open declarations for or against the current issues and use their influence with the "right persons or groups." The mayor as administrative head and an elective official is both relatively powerful as patronage dispenser, and exposed to pressure from citizens to whom he may be indebted for his position either in the past or in the future.

In contrast to this pattern, English City has a city council composed of 112 members drawn from 28 wards. Each ward elects four members. When the council is organized, members are appointed to committees that meet once or twice a week. Issues that arise in any part of the community are quickly brought to the council's attention. The city clerk is the administrative head of the city government. He is a civil servant appointed by the council on the basis of his administrative ability and serves under a requirement of impartiality as elections come and political parties change in power. The members of the council are released by their employers from work at the time of meetings. They are paid a stipend by the local government for time lost from work and for any personal expenses incurred in attending meetings within or outside the city. Table 4 shows the occupational composition of 110 members (2 vacant seats) of English City Council in 1955.

The council is composed of three major groups: trade union members form 32 per cent, business members 30 per cent, and other community members 37 per cent. Five of the twelve Key Influentials of the community are members and play major roles in their respective parties. The council is the major arena of community decision. Issues reach it directly, are investigated by council committees, and are decided upon by a vote taken in the full council. Community organizations play important roles in debating the issues, but these are definitely secondary or supplementary activities. The community value system condemns any pressure tactics on the council as "bad taste." However, in the council a caucus of elected party leaders is held before any important vote and a position is taken by the leaders for the party. The "whip" is applied and members are expected to vote as instructed. Such action is rationalized as necessary for responsible party government.

A different occupational prestige system and a different council-community power-complex, seem to explain the variation in the composition of Key Influentials who come to power in Pacific City from those in English City.

Another question: Do Key Influential leaders in a community influence policy-making by acting in concert through cliques?

Table 4. Occupational Composition of English City Council in 1955

32 Per Cent Trade Union Members N=37	30 Per Cent Business Group Members N=33	37 Per Cent Other Community Sectors N=40
2 Foremen	4 Manufacturers	2 Solicitors
16 Skilled workers	7 Wholesale and retail owners	1 Doctor
5 Semi-skilled workers	1 Cinema owner	1 Dentist
8 Clerical workers	4 Contractors	1 Engineer
4 Trade union officials	8 Company directors and secretaries	1 Accountant
2 Unskilled workers	1 Bank official	1 Auctioneer
		1 Teacher
		2 Ministers
		3 Political party organizing secretaries
		3 National government officials
		12 Housewives
		12 Retired workers

The identification of clique-structures is an extremely difficult undertaking. Many respondents will claim cliques exist simply because they have seen persons together many times or have heard that certain people were good friends. Hunter relied upon the mapping of certain sociometric relationships based on committee choices, on participation patterns of influentials in issues as described by them, and on specific statements of informants. The researcher would like to make direct observations of Key Influentials when they are acting in relation to community issues and perhaps, in other dealings with each other. Since this is almost impossible to obtain, cumulative indirect evidence is sought.

The test of the hypothesis in Pacific City relied upon the following kinds of evidence:[18]

1) Measures of group cohesiveness based on committee member selections of Key Influentials.

2) Acquaintance patterns of Top Influentials and Key Influentials.

3) Committee participation as reported by Top Influentials and Key Influentials.

4) Personal estimates of clique behavior among Top Influentials.

5) Activity of Key Influentials in community organizations.

6) Patterns of overlapping membership of Key Influentials in business, social, civic, and professional organizations.

7) Clique behavior and the dynamics of community decision making.

Table 5 is a matrix pattern of the overlapping membership of the Key Influentials in the business, civic, and social organizations of Pacific City. It shows that mutual contact is established between the Key Influentials in business, social and civic organizations, but the common participation established by the

---

[18] *Ibid.*, pp. 577-609.

small group who interact in the business sector may be the most significant. Three of the Key Influentials whom informants have designated as meeting together when there is a serious financial crisis or money-raising need are among those most active in the business sector.

There is a grand total of ninety-four overlapping business, social, and civic memberships among the twelve Key Influentials. The rank-order correlation between the policy committee choice rank and rank position based on the overlapping membership is .42. This indicates that a moderate correlation exists and suggests that group interaction may build common ties and leadership reputations.

Focused interviews of approximately one hour were conducted with each Top Influential and Key Influential and some carefully selected informants to probe for the basis of their opinion. Two patterned groupings emerge as the principal referents: a general pattern of fluid coalition among influentials is discerned about most issues; clique-relations are observed around a set of specific situations. It is this second pattern which evokes the belief that crowds exist and make the big decisions in Pacific City. A few interview comments are quoted to show these two patterns.

Interview Evidence for a General Pattern of Fluid Coalition

"There are no crowds as such. There are perhaps ten main leaders and the majority of them must be behind any major controversial issue in Pacific City to make it successful. There are probably thirty more persons, less active and less influential, who contribute their time and energy. I am not aware of any subgroups within this group of forty that cling together on issues generally." — A College President (Key Influential)

"There are a group of about thirty men who are primarily responsible for the major decisions in Pacific City. Quite frequently they are the 'second men' in important organizations who have both the approval of the top men and the youth and time to

TABLE 5

The Matrix of Overlapping Memberships of the 12 Key Influentials in Pacific City for Business, Social and Civic Organizations

Key Influentials of Pacific City	Investment E	Investment U	Insurance W	Insurance P	Real Estate Y	Bank F	Bank P	Bank W	Social Club	Business Club	Golf Club	Masonic Lodge	University Club	College Club	Golf Club	Tennis Club	Chamber of Commerce	United Good Neighbors	Rotary	Municipal League	Community Chest	World Affairs Council	Orthopedic Hospital	Total Number of Overlapping Memberships in Business, Social and Civic Organizations
D.D.	X	X	X		X	X			X	X	X	X			X		X	X	X	X			X	15
H.E.	X	X		X					X	X		X				X	X		X	X	X	X		12
O.R.	X	X	X	X					X	X	X						X	X	X				X	11
T.S.	X	X	X						X	X	X	X			X		X						X	10
L.A.						X	X		X	X	X		X				X		X					8
R.F.								X		X	X	X					X	X			X	X		8
B.B.					X			X	X		X						X	X	X					7
A.Y.							X		X	X		X					X	X						6
C.S.									X					X	X		X			X	X			6
E.L.									X	X						X	X	X						5
L.C.										X										X	X			3
W.O.													X							X	X			3

Total Number of Overlapping Membership in Business Organizations 21

Total Number of Overlapping Memberships in Social Organizations 37

Total Number of Overlapping Memberships in Civic Organizations 36

Grand Total All Overlapping Memberships 94

spend a large amount of time and energy on civic work. Many of the decisions are formulated informally in groups of two or three at social functions." — A Doctor (Top Influential)

"Pacific City has no rigid structure of leadership. No one person or one group runs the city. As issues appear various persons take sides and push for their view. Different coalitions appear on the issues. However, there is a small core of four leaders, all of them are good fund raisers and people and groups turn to them." — Veteran Newspaper Writer (Informant)

Interview Evidence for Clique Relations Around a Set of Specific Situations

" There are probably four groups in Pacific City who are stable and act as a group. The most influential one is the businessmen's group who are largely Republicans, active both in city and state affairs, members of the Chamber of Commerce, Municipal League, and active in school board elections. The second is the labor groups who act together on some issues. There is a third group which is composed mainly of Democrats. They have their own money. There is also a fourth group which unofficially stems from the Council of Churches but influences mainly through individual Protestant ministers. They are interested in the character of various political candidates and boosted the last governor." — A Republican Party Leader (Top Influential)

"There is no one crowd, but a key leader works through friends whom he respects and with whom he can get things done. Take this example for instance. The president of the Symphony Board wanted help on the symphony drive. I met with E.B. and S.B. and L.B. (all Key Influentials) in L.B.'s office. We sat around and talked about who should head up the drive. B.G.'s name was suggested. I was tagged to go with E.B. and hang the job on him. That's the way things get done—in informal meetings."

"Now in politics, there are ten of us who have gotten together and tried to see that a good man was selected for mayor. We picked T.N. and you could have gotten 100 to 1 that he would have been licked, but he won. Now I haven't been in the mayor's office since. We don't dictate."—A Business Leader (Key Influential)

"There are several recognizable blocs that usually present the same front. The Chamber of Commerce is probably the most important bloc both in initiating and in influencing. Labor is generally well organized. Educational groups are usually united on issues such as passage of school bond levies but are too divided to present any solid influential body. Welfare agencies shy away from expressions of opinion and are not opinion molders. Newspapers and radio are not influential in local issues."
—A Religious Leader (Key Influential)

"There are ten or twelve in the elite that make the big decisions. They are primarily in the business field and they work in cliques; the cliques are formed with a member of those ten or twelve and they delegate authority down to lesser influentials in their areas." — A Social Work Leader (Top Influential)

"There are five or six 'big men' who make most of the decisions; they are important through private and corporate wealth and property. They are socially cohesive, stable, and mostly Republicans, but that is not an important factor. They vote consistently together on issues and are mainly interested in only the important decisions. They are 'top level' operators. There is a second level group of about twenty-five who are mainly from business. Both the small and large groups are Chamber of Commerce members in part." — Lawyer and Former Mayor (Top Influential)

These opinions do not lend themselves to any simple consensus, but a scrutiny of all the behavior and attitudinal evidence leads us to rejection of the working hypothesis in the following respects:

1) Key Influentials do not repeatedly act in concert utilizing subordinate groups. There is no "crowd" pattern in

Pacific City and English City such as Hunter reports for Regional City. Regional City represents a more structured organization of the Top Influentials with ties to subordinate groups.

2) There are key leaders who bring various other influentials around them when they are responsible for getting a civic project carried out. These groupings do have a pattern and tend to be repeated because key leaders find they can work best with certain leaders and can get the job done. However, there is a significant degree of fluidity. Various leaders may be called upon for the responsible direction of policy making and different Key Influentials and Top Influentials may be drawn in. Both Pacific City and English City show a fluid core of 12-15 Key Influentials with up to 150 Top Influentials. Different combinations appear with different issues. No one person or group dominates.

SUMMARY AND INTERPRETATION

The three cities that have been studied are alike in many ways. There is a vigorous business leadership to be found in all three cities. There is a hierarchy of civic leadership in which various Key Influentials and Top Influentials have a "place." There are friendship groupings and patterns of common social and civic participation which bring people together. There is a large number of Top Influentials in all three cities, up to 100-150, who have a standing in the eyes of the total community and may be called upon for leadership services when a project is before the entire community.

The three cities that have been studied are different in many ways. English City does not look to its business leaders so much for civic leadership as do the two American cities. The business representation among the Key Influentials in Pacific City is 67 per cent; in Regional City, 75 per cent; in English City, 25 per cent. The solution of civic problems is carried on more directly by the city council in English City while voluntary organizations are more fluid and the solidarity of the Key Influentials is less in both English City and Pacific City than in Regional City.

What can one conclude from all of this evidence? Tentatively the following conclusions seem in order:

1) Businessmen are over-represented in the institutional distribution of community interests and do dominate community policy-making in most communities.

2) Local government is a relatively weak power-center. Opinion formation takes place within organized groups and influence is brought to bear upon the city council so that it functions as a subordinate of the dominant forces in the community power-structure.

3) The influence of certain persons, groups, and institutions is significantly curtailed and neutralized. This includes many corporate managers, professionals in government, education, religion, welfare, and mass communication.

4) Key Influentials are persons who are drawn from positions of first-rate power and influence. They are generally "economic dominants" in the community.[19] Although the majority live outside the city limits they do maintain an active interest in the central city.

THE RANGE OF COMMUNITY POWER-STRUCTURES

The evidence presented has now blunted some of the major indictments made earlier. The city has not lost most of its effective leaders. Tight inner clique groups are not found uniformly at the apex of community power-structures. The indictments charging the community with loss of social solidarity and physical identity rest upon probative evidence rather than upon

---

[19] Robert O. Schulze reports to the contrary for a suburban city. See Robert O. Schulze, "The Role of Economic Dominants in Community Power Structures," *American Sociological Review*, XXIII (February, 1958), 7-9. The withdrawal of "economic dominants" exhibited in Cibola was not demonstrated in Pacific City or English City. William H. Form and William V. D'Antonio report no such withdrawal in El Paso, Texas or C. Juarez, Mexico.

validated facts. However, the evidence for the charge that local government is a relatively weak power-center has been accumulating in a number of studies.

All conclusions about community power-structures must remain tentative until the range of power-structures is identified. Generalizations made about any community must be related to its appropriate power-structure type or model. A search for such models must begin with identification of significant community variables.

SIGNIFICANT COMMUNITY VARIABLES

Schulze has suggested that such ecological variations as central city, satellite, and suburb may be significant in delineating power-structures and processes.[20] There is good evidence that the less diversified the economic base of the community, the more clustered is the potential for power. The political homogeneity of a community also seems to be a contributing factor. The size of a community is another variable that is related to differences in power-structure and processes. A typology of power-models might enable the investigator to subsume a number of these variables. Five different power-models are suggested to enclose differences in power-structures of communities.

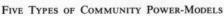

FIVE TYPES OF COMMUNITY POWER-MODELS

Model A is a pyramidal structure centering in one person. It is an autocratic form which may be identified in some company towns or one-industry towns or cities. This model is characterized by the fact that local political action, freedom of organizational affiliation including especially independent labor unionism, unbiased secular and perhaps even religious instruction, and indeed, the whole range of so-called civil liberties are either completely denied or effectively curtailed.[21] The local citizenry are

[20] Notes on Community Power Structure Conference, Harvard University, April 26-27, 1958.
[21] Wilbert E. Moore, *Industrial Relations and the Social Order* (New York: Macmillan, 1951), p. 556.

placed in the relatively fortunate or relatively unfortunate position (depending on the motive of the ruler) of vassals under a feudal overlord.

Model B is another pyramidal structure centering in a tightly-knit group of persons. It is an aristocracy which may be identified in a community where a family or small clique has gained control. The Lynds described Middletown as a community of this type. Here, the power of a wealthy family of manufacturers became hereditary with the emergence of a second generation of sons. One Middletown citizen described their pervasiveness in the following way: "If I'm out of work I go to X plant; if I need money I go to the X bank, and if they don't like me I don't get it; my children go to the X college; when I get sick I go to the X hospital; I buy a building lot or house in an X subdivision; my wife goes downtown to buy clothes at the X department store; if my dog strays away he is put in the X pound; I buy X milk; I drink X beer; vote for X political parties, and get help from X charities; my boy goes to the X YMCA and my girl to their YWCA. I listen to the word of God in X-subsidized churches; if I'm a Mason I go to the Masonic temple; I read the news from the X morning newspaper; and, if I'm rich enough, I travel via the X airport."[22]

It has been suggested that American small manufacturing cities could be classified into two groups — those in which the industrial pioneers or their sons still dominate the local business scene, and those in which "new blood" has taken over the leadership. There is high probability that the second group would be more prominent in cities having major industries. Model B differs from Model A in the fact that there is always the opportunity for other interests to challenge the existing power-structure. The fact that the company does not "own the whole town" means that other economic and social interests may assert them-

---

[22]   Robert S. Lynd and Helen M. Lynd, *Middletown in Transition* (New York: Harcourt, Brace, 1937), p. 74.

selves. The machinery for independent political action may be used for challenging company supremacy.

Model C, a stratified pyramidal structure, describes a community whose policy-making leaders are drawn largely from the business class. (See Figure 2.)

Model C

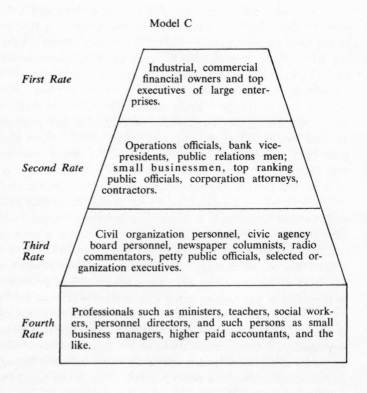

First Rate — Industrial, commercial financial owners and top executives of large enterprises.

Second Rate — Operations officials, bank vice-presidents, public relations men; small businessmen, top ranking public officials, corporation attorneys, contractors.

Third Rate — Civil organization personnel, civic agency board personnel, newspaper columnists, radio commentators, petty public officials, selected organization executives.

Fourth Rate — Professionals such as ministers, teachers, social workers, personnel directors, and such persons as small business managers, higher paid accountants, and the like.

Figure 2: Model C
*A Stratified Pyramidal Model of a Community Power-Structure
(after Hunter)*

In Regional City, an American city of the South, Floyd Hunter found that the business class formulated policy through cliques. On community-wide issues policy is channeled by a "fluid committee structure" down to institutionally associated groupings through a lower-level bureaucracy which executes policy. Intracommunity and extracommunity policy matters are handled by essentially the same group of (business) men in this city, but there is a differentiation of functional activity within this policy group. Finally, it was found that the structure is held together by common interests, mutual obligations, money, habit, delegated responsibilities, and in some cases by coercion and force.[23] There is reason to believe that this model fits an older, established community where the social system has been congenial to the growth of a social aristocracy and where business control has a history of hereditary growth. Indeed, Hunter points out that only fifteen of the forty top policy leaders gained positions of prominence on their own. All of the others inherited their father's business or were helped by the wealth and connections of their fathers. The model does not explain fully the community structure in English City. In the first place, similar evidence for cohesive crowds or cliques has not been found. To be sure, friendships existed but these are not utilized as a basis for unified common action on community issues. Secondly, there is a question as to whether the full scope of community power is to be found within the corps of leaders recognized as prominent in initiating or sanctioning actions having consequences for the community. There is some evidence that influence is increasingly centered within the hands of administration leaders who are responsible for large organizations within their own responsibility. Many unobtrusive leaders may exist whose influence through wealth, social status, and political power needs to be taken into account.

Model D, the ring or cone structure, best fits the pattern of

[23]   Hunter, *op. cit.,* p. 113.

the power-structure operating in many modern communities. It is characterized by three major qualities:

1) *Increasing heterogeneity of interests within the business sector:*

   a Certain manufacturers and merchants view expansion as a threat to labor supply and wage level.

   b Rise of managers brings a new caution and results in many leaders playing a neutral role.

   c Financial and property ties grow more complex as outside interests enter. Branch businesses increase; community improvements seem to some to be assets, to others, tax liabilities.

2) *Rise of new power structures:*

   a Labor leaders have come to have an ever stronger voice as agents of their own organization; labor becomes more educated and participates more broadly in community organizations, especially in political parties, government, and welfare organizations. A share in decision-making in the community is more easily attained by citizens of low status.

   b Political and government leaders are exercising greater infuence over more activities of community life. Military leadership has been given even greater responsibility.

   c Educational leaders command greater attention as the need for specialized personnel increases.

   d Society leaders may not be neglected in some communities, especially in New England and many European countries.

   e Major business leaders are being recruited for managerial talent rather than from hereditary and exclusively educated classes.

3) *Growing autonomy in all institutionalized sectors:*

   a Large-scale organization is growing in all sectors.

b Power of administration and policy-making is increasingly concentrated within the specialized personnel of the ✕
organization.

A test of the model can be made by discovering the range of
leadership displayed in the community and the nature of the
participation of various leaders in important decisions affecting
their organization, the institutional sector, or other local institutions. It is assumed that leaders play a number of different
roles, sometimes taking positive action, sometimes negative, often
remaining neutral, and even withdrawing completely from various issues. Different leaders are drawn into community issues
depending on the issue at stake.[24]

Figure 3 is a graphic illustration of those persons in English
City who were ranked as having the highest personal influence
over policy-making affecting the community. The ring structure
shows the range of institutional representatives. The area of each
segment is an approximation of the relative power of each segment as judged by the choice rank of the Top Influentials and by
panel raters who were asked to review the strength of each institutional area in securing desired outcomes on a number of
community issues. Those persons whose influence is greatest are
shown toward the center of the circle. Note the representatives
from the Labour party, the trade union and consumer co-opera-
tives, the Citizens party, business, civic organizations, religion,
education, and society. There is *no single cohesive elite structure
and no hierarchical dominance based on one institutional sector*.
The pattern of personal influence is best described as a kaleido-
scope of recognizable faces shifting in and out of fluid coalitions
as issues change.

While the cone or ring model is most appropriate for English
City, the stratified pyramid, with its solidary top business elite

[24] Delbert C. Miller, "Decision-Making Cliques in Community
Power Structures: A Comparative Study of an American and an
English City," *American Journal of Sociology,* LXIV (November,
1958), 309-310.

such as Hunter describes for Regional City, is also a useful guide to the power potential in Pacific City. However, Pacific City shows markedly more fluidity among both the Key and Top Influentials as issues change. Religion and education have a more influential role, as Pacific City numbers a college president and an Episcopalian bishop among its key influentials.

A continuum of community power-structures is suggested for large cities ranging from the highly stratified pyramid dominated by a small but powerful business group functioning through cliques of high solidarity to a ring of institutional representatives functioning in relatively independent roles. We have said that Regional City, Pacific City, and English City range in the order named along such a continuum.

A study of Lorain, Ohio, by James B. McKee verifies many features of Model D. He says: "No one group can now be called a ruling group in industrial society. This is so for two reasons. First, there is no single locus of decision-making, but rather a number of loci, each differently structured. Within the corporation is one, within the community are several, and there are other significant ones within the larger society. Second, a number of groups may have varying effects upon decision making in a given locus. Hence the *pyramidical model of the social order, with power and authority located at the apex, is inaccurate and misleading.*"[25]

Model E. consists of *segemented power pyramids*. When political parties are powerful in organizing leaders into two or more cohesive groups, the power-structure of a community may be described as political blocs. In one English city there was

[25]   James B. McKee, "Status and Power in the Industrial Community: A Comment on Drucker's Thesis," *American Journal of Sociology* (January, 1953), p. 369. See Donald W. Olmsted, "Organizational Leadership and Social Structure in a Small City," *American Sociological Review* (June, 1954), pp. 273-81; Roland J. Pellegrin and Charles H. Coates, "Absentee-Owned Corporations and Community Power Structure," *American Journal of Sociology* (March, 1956), pp. 413-20.

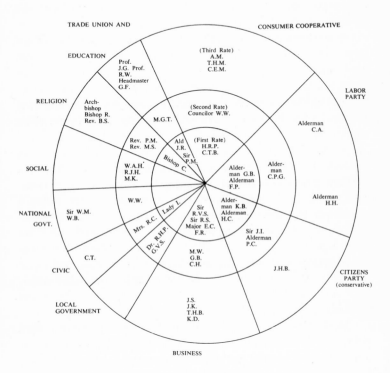

Figure 3. Model D:
*An Institutional Ring or Cone Structure of Top Influentials in
English City*

considerable evidence for this kind of political model. On all important issues there is a caucus of the Labour and Conservative power leaders, decisions for voting action are taken, and the whip is applied to all members to vote in conformance with the decision of the caucus. Community power breaks cleanly along party lines.

Other arrangements are possible within the segmented model. Splinter groups may form a whole series of multiple-power pyramids with a great deal of cleavage between them. French politics reflect the contours of such a model.

The research we need may not be sufficient to draw many firm conclusions but questions stubbornly do assert themselves.

There remains, however, the final question to be answered, and which has dominated this entire discussion: Have we achieved democratic community life? Is community life strong enough to solve our problems, accomplish our aspirations, and make us proud of our democratic way of life? Surely, most observers would have to be honest enough to say that when our achievements are compared to our ideals, the results do not measure up to them.

How can we work toward improvement of the local community? How can we reconstruct community power-structures?

THE RECONSTRUCTION OF COMMUNITY POWER-STRUCTURES IN A DEMOCRATIC SOCIETY

There would appear to be nothing that would affect community life more than to open wide many old and many new channels in and through the community power-structure. The goal of proportional representation for all the institutional segments of our society is in the democratic tradition. A planning committee, for instance, should have the full range of the relevant interests of the community—artist and scholar, politician and minister, businessman and housewife. If each issue and project could be tackled by such a balanced power-structure, the decisions would have different casts. As opportunities to participate are broadened and more persons learn the skills of decision-making, silence and pessimism might be quickly reversed. The erasure of fear among current policy-makers must certainly constitute the major hurdle. Top business leaders fear that ill-advised persons will make unwise economic decisions. In fact, many businessmen feel that they are the natural leaders of the community because they understand the economic facts of life and believe that any transfer or sharing of leadership will bring disaster.

Kurt Lewin, the late psychologist who fled Europe, told us that democracy is truly a way of thinking. Until democratic thinking actually suffuses the heart of the community, power-structure progress will be slow. It is obvious, however, that many groups have never marshalled their potential power. New power-groups can and do rise. In time they win their place in the power-structure. Meanwhile, they have the single most precious political right that any person can possess. With an equal vote, the power of influence, indeed, of revolutionary influence, rests with those who will exercise their right. I have observed in the State of Washington how a group of laboring people joined by the Catholic Church and with the support of an opposing political party brought defeat to a right-to-work initiative which had been supported heavily by Top and Key Influentials. This is the kind of manifestation which tells all of us, whether we are on the winning or losing side of an issue, that democracy is alive and as viable as the American community. It is a force which often moves with slowness. Great potentials of democratic sentiment lie about untapped and unused. But the power of democracy is there and, if preserved, new generations can always be challenged to improve in its exercise. The face and character of the community will reveal to all who will look what success the people have achieved in translating dreams into reality.

Professor Robert A. Dahl, Eugene Meyer
Professor and Chairman of the Political Science
Department at Yale University, has worked
for several governmental agencies, as well as
for the U.S. Group Control Council, which
functioned in Germany after the Second World War.
He is the author of *Congress and Foreign Policy,*
Domestic Control of Atomic Energy
(with Ralph S. Brown, Jr.),
Politics, Economics and Welfare
(with Charles E. Lindblom), and
A Preface to Democratic Theory.

3

EQUALITY AND POWER
IN AMERICAN
SOCIETY

Robert A. Dahl

Perhaps the best way to begin my exploration of equality and power in American society is to indicate some of my differences with Professor Miller. First of all, I disagree with most of his indictments of the local community. I disagree, not because I think there is no truth in his charges, but because I think they are only a part of the truth. Thus I disagree with the hypothesis that the local community has *lost* its social solidarity because I do not know that it ever *had* social solidarity. As I look back on the history of New Haven, Connecticut, I ask myself: When was New Haven a solidary community? When was New Haven that great Utopia, a nonstratified, highly solidary community that is apparently in the minds of people who say that social solidarity has declined? What is the evidence for a change?

Throughout its lengthy history, New Haven has been torn by disputes. The patrician, Congregationalist, upper-class oligarchy that ran New Haven for the first two centuries of its life was not, as I should have expected if I accepted this hypothesis as fact, a body of leaders that stimulated a high degree of solidarity and unity in the community; indeed, in due course of time when the common people got the opportunity they promptly tossed out this body of leaders. I find no evidence that nineteenth-century capitalism and industrialism — which spawned a proletariat and induced a great influx of immigrant groups who often suffered from meager incomes, low status, limited education, and difficulties in assimilating themselves — produced a particularly unified community. If anything, I would propose that there is as much solidarity in New Haven now as there has ever been. In sum, what is the evidence that New Haven, or other American communities, enjoyed *more* solidarity in earlier times?

I would also question the charge that the community has lost its most effective leaders. If by its most effective leaders we mean men of wealth and social status, then this is true by definition; but if we mean men of imagination, daring, force, enterprise and skill, I think there is no convincing evidence that we are worse off than we have been. Again, I have to ask — what is this assertion based upon? Who were the leaders of the American communities in the first half of the twentieth century? Were the leaders in American towns and cities really so very remarkable in the nineteenth century? Only a short time ago, New York produced a Fiorello LaGuardia; or consider Richardson Dilworth and Joseph Clark in Philadelphia, Daley in Chicago, Lawrence in Pittsburgh, Lee in New Haven — men like these compare favorably with any city leadership that we have had over the past century and a half. To be sure, except for Dilworth and Clark in Philadelphia, these new men have not had the benefits of a university education; they have made their way up in the world, they did not come out of the upper social classes, they do not have great wealth. But they are men of talent, they are men of enterprise, and they are men of strength. Therefore, I wonder whether compared with previous times, there has been such a notable decline in leadership in our communities.

Next, is it true that our local political institutions are weak? I don't think it is valid to compare the City Council of New Haven or the City Council of Chicago with the City Council of English City. There are other comparisons that one ought to make. One ought to ask how many people vote in elections in English City? I don't know anything about English City, but in many local elections in England only 10 to 20 per cent of the adult population votes. Is this a sign of the strength of political institutions in England? Is this a sign that democracy is working better there? For a valid comparison, we should also compare the executives in the two systems. In the United States, the chief executive is typically the mayor, and a great increase has been taking place in the power and vigor of the mayor in many American communities.

Now consider the charge that power rests with a small inner circle of leaders who operate *outside* of the official governing bodies. Fear, pessimism, and silence, it is said, dominate the community's social climate; this is certainly not true of any community that I ever lived in. Many critics of the American community expect that there *must* be a monolithic structure of some kind, a monolithic structure run either by "good guys" or by "bad guys." Consequently, when one discovers that the local community is in pretty bad shape, which it is, then the only inference that one can make is that it is run by the evil elements. Now if you look for a monolithic structure in any community, or in any human organization, and if you look only at the evidence that suggests a monolith, then you will almost certainly find a monolith. Yet despite countless variations, I don't think that the typical American community *is* a monolithic but rather a pluralistic system. We need to learn how to recognize, how to analyze, and how to work with pluralistic systems. I would contend that in most American communities there isn't a single center of power. There is even a sense in which *nobody* runs the community. In fact, perhaps this is the most distressing discovery of all: typically a community is run by many different people, in many different ways, at many different times.

Next, I doubt very much whether businessmen "dominate" community policies, except perhaps by definition. What policies? Fund-raising? If one means fund-raising, then this is so. New Haven, like most communities, has a community fund drive that is carried on mainly by young businessmen who are looking for a chance to make a mark as go-getters and to pick up some recognition and prestige. But what about public schools? Have these been dominated by businessmen? In New Haven they are "dominated" by other groups. What about police? What about the welfare programs themselves, that is, the decisions about what's done with the money raised by the businessmen or by taxes? In my community these welfare groups are dominated by the professionals, who make decisions mainly by lobbying with one another on a council of social agencies. What can be said about charter reform? There have been businessmen in communities all over the United States, who year after year have tried to change the city charter; one would suppose that if they were a dominant elite, by now they would have achieved the kind of charter they want. But for the most part, I think, cities tend to have the kinds of charters that politicians want. What of urban redevelopment? If there is anything in the community in which businessmen are involved it is urban redevelopment. Yet by and large the businessmen do not even "dominate" urban redevelopment. It is the strong executive, Mayor Dilworth or Mayor Lee, who provides the leadership on redevelopment.

Finally, I entertain very serious doubts about the methods and the conceptual apparatus on which Professor Miller's conclusions rest. I believe that his evidence does not lead to his conclusions. For a _reputation_ for power is not necessarily a valid index of power. An alternative way to determine who "runs things" is to study a series of concrete decisions in order to find out who specifically dominates those decisions. If this is done, you may or may not find a correlation with reputations. In talking with a good many businessmen in New Haven I have found that even with respect to decisions in which they have participated, often they are extremely vague as to what actually transpired.

Moreover, no proposition about power or influence has much meaning unless one specifies power or influence with respect to something: power over public schools, over fund-raising, over redevelopment, over the local police, in the courts, or what? If

76

these different sectors are specified, probably in many communities people who are influential with respect to one sector are not terribly influential with respect to another; and <u>individuals influential in one sector may come out of different socioeconomic strata from those who are influential in another.</u> Finally, I should like to suggest a simple test. We know from public opinion polls and other research that large businessmen, in the main, are Republicans and that they are very anxious for Republican candidates to win. Now if they are the *dominant* power in a community, it should follow, I should think, that they would be able to win elections. If they can't, then I don't know what the word *dominant* means. Therefore, one test is to see what happens in the presidential elections. Which candidate will carry the cities — that is, the communities where businessmen are said to be "dominant"? I should think that if businessmen are "the dominant power institution in the United States" then the election is already foreclosed. Yet we know that the 106 cities with populations over 100,000 have been the stronghold of the Democratic Party. In 1936, Franklin Roosevelt carried 104 out of these 106 cities — in 1940, 97. How does this square with Professor Miller's conclusion? Did businessmen *want* Roosevelt to win? If not, and if they *dominate* these communities, why can't they win in a really critical trial of strength such as the elections of 1936 and 1940 surely were? Do candidates backed by business regularly win elections for mayor? Do business proposals regularly win on referenda? If not, how can we conclude that businessmen "dominate"? Isn't there something faulty in Miller's analysis?

With the differences between Miller and me as a preface, let me turn now to another interpretation of certain problems of American communities — problems created by their failure to measure up to the exacting demands of democratic ideals.

My emphasis, however, will be on *appraisal* rather than on description or explanation. What I want to evaluate are the distribution and patterns of influence over political decisions in

American life. I shall lean heavily on New Haven for information on the distribution and patterns of influence, but I do so in the belief that New Haven is similar to many other communities and strikingly similar in many ways to the United States as a whole. Where there are differences, I shall try to take these into account.

To appraise, one needs standards of appraisal, criteria of performance, values. Many different criteria are relevant to the task of arriving at an appraisal of the distribution and patterns of influence. I propose, however, to concern myself with only one, the criterion of political equality. Obviously, other criteria might also be invoked. I will not attempt here to justify my choice of equality, except to say that it is a value that has always been a salient aspect of democratic beliefs.

When one examines a political decision — that is, a decision determining the policies enforced by governmental officials — or what persons become officials — one usually finds that for any particular sector of policy only a small number of persons ever initiate alternatives or veto the proposals of others. These individuals are leaders or policy-makers. One may say that they have the greatest *direct* influence on decisions. A larger number of persons, subleaders, generally have moderate influence. But most citizens usually have little or no *direct* influence in this sense: they never initiate or veto any alternatives.

One is also likely to find, however, that some leaders are extremely sensitive to the attitudes and preferences of individuals and groups who do not directly initiate or veto alternatives. Often this indirect influence is *anticipatory*: a leader initiates or vetoes a particular alternative because he anticipates rewards for choosing from one set of alternatives, or sanctions if he chooses from a different set. In this way, persons or groups who are not leaders may exert great indirect influence on the choice of alternatives even though they never directly initiate or veto.

In New Haven, for example, the present mayor has not until this present year ever advocated an increase in taxes, although he has done almost everything else to raise money. Why has he not tried to increase taxes? It was not, I think, because someone said, "Mayor Lee, don't you dare raise taxes!" For the mayor grew up in New Haven; he knows enough about the city to know that raising taxes is politically risky. He *anticipated* what might happen to him in the next election if he should raise taxes. If the decision to take the risk is made, at least it is a fact that the risk involved has been anticipated.

Indirect influence, which is often anticipatory in character, is very important for some kinds of leaders, particularly those who have to win elections. Yet even when indirect influence of this sort is taken into account, the distribution of influence in most sectors of policy is very far indeed from the perfect equality that some democratic theorists would regard as ideal.

One of the main reasons why the system does not very closely approximate political equality is the unequal distribution of access to political resources — that is, to inducements of all kinds. One's influence is partly a function of the political resources to which one has access — labor time, money and credit, jobs, information, popularity, wealth, social standing, legality, and the like. An examination of any one of these political resources will show that some persons have much greater access to it than others. So long as this is the case, political equality is not likely to be approximated. This is hardly a novel conclusion, for a great many writers on politics have said in one way or another that a high degree of equality in the distribution of political resources is a necessary — though by no means a sufficient — condition for a high degree of equality of control over political decisions. This was, for example, one of Tocqueville's key propositions in his analysis of democracy in America.

In appraising inequality in political resources, it is important not to make the mistake of assuming that what we are trying to judge is a ruling elite masquerading in the name of democracy. For if citizens do not rule the system as political equals neither does a unified elite control decisions, at least not in New Haven. There may be exceptions in specific communities, but I am inclined to think that most cities and states, and certainly the national government, are in this respect rather like New Haven.

To condemn our political system for inequality is one thing; to condemn it for being dominated by a ruling elite is another. In my view, appraisal is infinitely more complicated, precisely because the political system is neither a democracy in which citizens share equally in all important decisions nor an oligarchy ruled by an elite. Rather, it combines elements of both.

In the American system (insofar as New Haven is a fair prototype), though political equality is certainly not attained and political resources are unequally distributed, democracy is not wholly subverted into oligarchy because the growth of oligarchy is inhibited both by the *patterns* according to which political resources are allocated and by the ways in which resources are actually *used*.

Let me try to make my point clearer first by some abstract considerations on the nature of power and influence. Abstractly, there is no reason to assume that the relative influence different individuals or groups exert on the decisions of one another is simply and solely a funtion of the "size" of their resources, that is, of the inducements they have at their disposal.

In the first place, an individual need not *use* his political resources to gain direct or indirect influence over officials of government. To be sure, the extent to which one is willing to use his political resources for political ends, depends *in part* on the magnitude of his resources; for example a millionaire who contributed $100 to a political campaign gives up fewer alternative opportunities than a poor man. But the extent to which a person uses his political resources will depend on other factors as well, including his confidence in the success of his effort, the extent to which he has alternative ways of gaining his ends other than through politics, and the extent to which he expects he will be benefited or injured by government policies. In New Haven, we have found variations attributable to each of these factors.

For example, Negroes in New Haven, a minority of probably 10 or 12 per cent of the population, operate at a much higher level of political participation than any other single isolated group in the community. What is the reason for this? The political arena is one area where Negroes are not thwarted and blocked by substantial discrimination. They can get jobs, patronage, and city contracts; they have their votes; their votes are legitimate, and they are counted; and so it has been for a century. This isn't true in the other sectors of community life; so Negroes work harder in the political arena to compensate for their disadvantages.

In the second place, one individual may use his political resources more *skillfully* than another — a variation known to students of politics for several centuries. By a skillful use of limited resources, in fact, a political entrepreneur — Machiavelli's Prince — can increase his resources and thus his influence.

In the third place, the relative influence of different potential coalitions will depend in part on the extent to which individuals and groups actually *combine* their resources. The combined political resources of a very numerous group of individuals who are not very well off may easily exceed the combined political resources of a small elite, each member of which is, individually, very well off. The extent to which people in a group actually combine their resources depends, of course, on the degree of political unity among them. There is no a priori reason for supposing that the rich will display more unity than the poor; and even if they do, it does not follow that the combined resources of the well-off strata will inevitably exceed the combined resources of the badly-off strata of a society.

Now, when we turn from these abstract considerations to the way in which different kinds of inducements — political resources — are actually distributed in New Haven we discover that a most significant change seems to have taken place during the last century and a half. In 1800, the citizens of New Haven were not only very unequal in access to political resources of

81

all kinds but their inequalities were *cumulative*. That is, the same tiny elite possessed the highest social standing, wealth, dominance in economic affairs, superior education, control over educational and religious institutions, a monopoly of public offices, evidently a large measure of legitimacy, and perhaps (though this is more doubtful) even popularity. Today, however, inequalities that exist with respect to all these resources tend to be noncumulative or *dispersed*. I can find no single elite at the top of the heap; instead there are many different varieties of political resources, with a somewhat different elite at the top of each. I am inclined to think that this pattern is not peculiar to New Haven but is common throughout the United States, though one would doubtless find exceptions to it here and there.

Moreover, I am tempted toward the hypothesis that the pattern of dispersed inequalities is a likely product of an advanced industrial society, at least if it operates with the kinds of political institutions that most of us would call democratic. The impact of Marx and Weber on habits of thought about industrial society has been very great, even among non-Marxists and non-Weberians, and both men lead us to expect that an advanced industrial society will be rather neatly and consistently stratified along lines shaped by economic class or bureaucratic position. I believe we should entertain the hypothesis that any industrial society in an advanced stage enters on a profound change that can be held back, if at all, only by a most vigorous and oppressive centralized regime. In a moderately free political system, at this stage, increasing affluence, widespread education, impersonal standards of recruitment, incredible specialization of functions and skills, the varieties of popularity, prestige, and achievement, standardization of consumer goods, social and geographical mobility, and probably many other factors, all tend to produce a pattern of dispersed rather than cumulative inequalities. The advance of industrial society may somewhat reduce inequalities in political resources; it does not, however, erase them. Nonetheless, in New Haven, and I think in American society generally, these inequalities are no longer cumulative.

To the extent that inequalities persist, tendencies toward oligarchy also exist in advanced industrial societies. But to the extent that inequalities are dispersed rather than cumulative — as I am suggesting they are in the United States — the growth of a unified oligarchy is inhibited. For the pattern of dispersed inequalities means that an individual or a group at a disadvantage with respect to one resource may compensate for his handicap by exploiting his superior access to a different resource. In New Haven, for example, for the past half century men whose main political resources were popularity and ethnic solidarity have been able to win elections. Very few individuals or groups in New Haven, and I believe this to be true in the United States, are totally lacking in political resources *of some kind*.

The possibility of turning to alternative kinds of resources would be less significant if one kind of resource — say wealth or social standing — dominated all the others, in the sense that a person or group superior in the one resource would invariably exert superior influence in a conflict with persons who drew on other political resources. Yet — and this is the second great limit on the growth of oligarchy — this is simply not the case, despite a tradition of economic determinism that runs in a straight line from Madison to Veblen, Beard, the Lynds, and C. Wright Mills. Surely if the New Deal demonstrated anything, it proved that leaders with popularity and votes can — even if they do not always do so — carry out their policies despite the opposition of leaders supported by men of wealth and social standing. This is a point that was perfectly obvious to both Aristotle and Tocqueville, who considered the problem in the light of observations made on radically different sorts of political systems.

In the third place, individuals or groups who are at a disadvantage in their access to resources can sometimes compensate by using their resources at a relatively high level. In New Haven, Negroes who, as I said before, are more active politically than any other identifiable ethnic group in the city, have overcome some of the disadvantages imposed by their incomes, status, and occupations.

Fourth, an individual or group at a disadvantage in resources may compensate by developing a high level of political skill. Fortunately the skills required in electioneering and party politics are by no means a monopoly of any stratum in the community; one might even conclude that leaders drawn from the well-to-do tend to be somewhat less likely to develop these skills to a high peak of proficiency than leaders drawn from the less-well-off strata of the community. In fact, many sorts of politicking run more sharply counter to the norms of the upper strata than of the lower or lower-middle strata.

Fifth, a group of citizens each of whom is weak in political resources may compensate by combining resources so that in the aggregate these are formidable. One resource that can be most easily aggregated by the less-well-off strata is the ballot. In New Haven, historically the least well-off citizens in the community have been Negroes and members of various immigrant groups whose circumstances produce a unity at the polls that declines as assimilation progresses. This unity among the poor has enabled them — or more accurately, perhaps, their leaders — to influence nominations, elections, and policies (often, to be sure, covert rather than overt policies) despite their lowly status, their low incomes, and their poverty in many other political resources.

Sixth, competitive elections insure that elected officials attempt to shape their covert and overt policies so as to win elections, hence to maximize votes, or at any rate to gain more votes than any rival. Consequently, whenever the many are believed to hold views on government policies at odds with the views held among the few, there exists one set of persons, elected politicians, who are strongly impelled to win votes by shaping or seeming to shape governmental policies according to the views of the many.

The system would be easier to judge either if it did not fall so far short of the goal of political equality — or, ironically, if it fell much shorter than it does. In the first case one might conclude that we possess a reasonable approximation of political equality, and approve the fact; in the other, one might conclude that we have an oligarchy, and condemn it roundly. But in my view the facts do not permit either judgment.

Some of you might draw comfort from the belief that the American system, if I have described it rightly, comes close to the mixture of democracy and oligarchy that Aristotle concluded was "the best constitution and the best way of life for the *majority* of states and men," and which he called a polity. I cannot forbear quoting here a few lines from Barker's translation of *The Politics*.

> . . . It is a good criterion of a proper mixture of democracy and oligarchy that a mixed constitution should be able to be described indifferently as either. . . . A properly mixed 'polity' should look as if it contained both democratic and oligarchical elements — and as if it contained neither. It should owe its stability to its own intrinsic strength, and not to external support; and its intrinsic strength should be derived from the fact, not that a majority are in favor of its continuance . . . , but rather that there is no single section in all the state which would favor a change to a different constitution. . . . It is clear from our argument, first, that the best form of political society is one where power is vested in the middle class, and secondly, that good government is attainable in those states where there is a large middle class — large enough, if possible, to be stronger than both of the other classes, but at any rate large enough to be stronger than either of them singly. *(pp. 177, 178, 180)*

You will recall also Aristotle's observation that polities of this kind were in fact rather rare, because in most states the middle class was small, and both the masses and the rich sought to install the constitution most favorable to them, either democracy or oligarchy.

For those who do not want to yield up the marvelous Utopian objective that animated the Declaration of Independence and the Gettysburg address, Aristotle's words will scarcely give complete comfort. Unless we abandon the ideal of political equality, and with it the American Dream, I do not see how we can live comfortably with the inequalities of power and political resources that we find around us. Can anyone who holds democratic beliefs remain satisfied with the American political system simply because it is not an oligarchy?

Unfortunately, however, solutions to the problem of political inequality are not as simple as they may have seemed to many hopeful democrats a century or more ago. In order to eliminate large inequalities in direct influence on governmental policies we should have to make far-reaching, indeed revolutionary, alterations in the character of modern society, such as the destruction of the national state and the elimination of all forms of bureaucratic organization including the business corporation. It would also require a world at peace. Even then, so long as individuals had different motives, interests, and skills, sizable differences in direct influence undoubtedly would appear. I do not believe that enough people are interested in these changes — which would generate their own train of uncertainties and impose great costs to other values we all hold — to make it worth the effort to explore them here, even though attempts to think through these problems realistically should continue.

Nor should one be misled by glib solutions. It might be argued, for example, that if inequalities in direct influence are inevitable, at least we should insure that there is equal opportunity to *gain* influence. Many persons are handicapped in the contest for office and influence by inequalities in resources that can be reduced, such as handicaps stemming from gross differences in income and inherited wealth, handicaps arising from inadequate opportunities for education, and handicaps arising from discriminatory practices based on race, ethnic group, religion, or social class. To the extent that these are remediable, surely we should not rest on our oars until the race is won.

But we must not be beguiled into assuming that equality of opportunity to *gain* influence will produce equality of *influence*. In fact, we are reducing and probably in the future will reduce even more many old inequalities in opportunities. But this merely insures that individuals will start out more or less even in a race for unequal influence. Even a modern dictatorship can achieve that. In fact some dictatorships seem to do a tolerably good job of it. It might be thought, too, that inequalities in direct influence over government policies could be reduced solely to *legitimate* differences in the relative influence of government officials, particularly elected officials, and ordinary citizens. No one, I suppose, would quarrel with the proposition that the President or the Secretary of State should have much greater influence over foreign policies, because of official position, than any other citizen. Yet it would be misleading to suppose that we are likely to reach a state of affairs in which reality corresponds to the simple model of democratic representation whereby appointive officials are merely the agents of elected officials, and elected officials are merely the agents of the majority. For in many sectors of policy, including most of the highly critical ones, elected and appointive officials have enormous leeway; public opinion and voting often provide only the vaguest sort of guide as to what is preferred by or even acceptable to a majority of voters. Views are often highly plastic: it is not so much the elected officials who are the agents of a majority as the other way round — voters wait for their trusted leaders to indicate what lines of policy should be followed.

If we are not likely — at least in the present state of national and world organization — to reduce very greatly the enormous differences that now exist with respect to direct influences on government policies, the problem of indirect influence is somewhat more manageable. The most promising means for providing an equal though indirect influence on policies is, surely, through participation in nominations, campaigns, and elections. Here the situation strikes me as a very hopeful one, for political self-confidence and participation are so much a function of education that the wide diffusion of educational opportunities is likely to reduce to insignificance many of the differences in political participation that stem from socioeconomic position rather than differences in personality. (Perhaps it is just as well that the differences in personality still elude control.)

Even in the case of campaigns and elections, however, wide participation is no cure-all. A formidable problem arises because of the enormous differences in opportunities for influencing the voters themselves. The problem is much more serious at the national than at the local level, for it is incomparably more expensive and more difficult to obtain a national hearing than a local one. Political theory has barely been extended to cover this problem; in particular, liberal democratic theory has often started with the assumption that the preferences of individuals, whether voters or consumers, should be taken as given, as autonomous to the individual rather than socially determined. To be sure, Tocqueville, Mill, and Bryce all looked beyond the individual to the towering influence of majority opinion on the views of the individual; and critics at the right and left have looked beyond the majority to the influence on its opinions wielded by key minorities of wealth, status and skill. There have been some innovations, like equal time, and more recently the famous TV debates between the presidential candidates. But clearly we have barely begun to grapple with this problem.

There can be no doubt, then, that our political system falls far short of the high standards of performance indicated by the criterion of political equality. No one who places a high value on political equality can afford to be complacent about the achievements of the American political system.

Nonetheless, it is misleading in the extreme to interpret the inequalities of power that mark our political life as signs of oligarchy. For in our system of dispersed inequalities, almost every group, as said before, has access to some resources that it can exploit to gain influence. Consequently, any group that feels itself badly abused is likely to possess both the resources it needs to halt the abuse and the incentive to use these resources at a high enough level to bring about changes. Nearly every group has enough potential influence to mitigate harsh injustice to its members, though not necessarily enough influence to attain a full measure of justice. The system thus tends to be self-corrective, at least in a limited fashion. If equality and justice are rarely attained, harsh and persistent oppression is almost always avoided. To this extent, the system attains one of the important ends of political equality without the means.

Professor Howard J. Ehrlich holds a dual appointment at The Ohio State University, serving in the Columbus Psychiatric Institute and Hospital as a Research Associate, and as Assistant Professor of Sociology in the Department of Sociology and Anthropology.
Intensive study in the fields of sociological theory and minority group behavior has occupied much of Dr. Ehrlich's time. He is presently completing a book on the Image of the Police in Contemporary Society.

4

POWER AND DEMOCRACY:
A CRITICAL DISCUSSION

Howard J. Ehrlich

The purpose of this chapter is to bring the three contributors together for a critical discussion of their respective views on power and democracy. The discussion which followed the presentation was led by Professor Howard J. Ehrlich. Professor Ehrlich proceeded to delineate and evaluate the major themes in the papers of Dahl, Drucker and Miller. He then addressed specific questions to the discussants relevant to these themes and each of the discussants responded to the questions and to the points raised by the other discussants.

Ehrlich — I shall exercise my prerogative as discussant not by discussing all three papers individually, but by looking at the central problems that they raise.

The first of these problems is the *question of conceptualizing power*. To begin with, "power" is a generic concept of social science — a facet of all human endeavors. Though we are here concerned with "political power," we ought to realize that such a limitation might well constrict the development of general theory and meaningful research design.

One of our first problems within this focus is that of specifying the relationships that obtain between power as a potential for action and power as a determinant of action itself. We know that the holders of positions of potential power are not necessarily those who exercise their power in national or community decisions. It has become apparent, moreover, that the study of political power must be focused about the *issues* under contention and the institutional sectors of those persons or groups who seek, legitimately or illegitimately, to control the decision-making processes. I shall have more to say about this below.

Related to this concern — but not developed by the members of this panel — is what I shall call the "issue of power challenge." By means of setting the stage for presentation of this issue, we need to emphasize two dimensions of American social life. First, we place a high premium on conformity. Second, and obviously related, is the trend, noted by both Dahl and Miller, of institutions and special-interest groups toward taking neutral positions on controversial community issues.

The fact that a given group does not exercise its power-potential under existing social conditions does not mean *ipso facto* that it has not been potent in the decision-making process. The sheer fact of the possession of a power-potential or resource may have been sufficient to determine the actions of others. But we *do* react to the potential power of another, and we *do* attempt to avoid the fearful showdown, the distasteful controversy, by anticipating the reactions of those in possession of power and by acting accordingly. There is thus no reason for those who hold a power-potential to exercise their power unless, and only unless, their domains are directly challenged. I fail to see how the members of this panel have taken into account, in their own research, this complex relationship between power as a potential for control and power as control itself. Although Dahl's analysis of what he calls "anticipatory influence" does touch upon this problem, it is by no means sufficient and I should like to hear from all members of the panel on this issue.

My second question is a *question of ideological focus*. Two alternative strategies have been manifest in contemporary political sociology. On the one hand, one may begin his inquiry by raising the question: Who has the power and what special or selfish interests are being served by its exercise? On the other hand, one may initiate inquiry on the basis of how given power-arrangements come to be developed, and what communal or societal functions are being served by the operation of such an arrangement. Put another way, one may focus on conflict and cleavage, or one may focus on integration and function. Clearly, the selection of either strategy is reflective of one's prior ideological commitment, and determinative of the sorts of data one will seek. For Miller and Drucker, the perspective is that of conflict and cleavage, for Dahl, that of integration and function. It is of interest here that not only does Dahl's paper stand in sharp opposition to the others, but that even Miller and Drucker, utilizing a similar strategy, fail to agree on basic issues. I think that the question of ideological commitment ought to be brought to the fore; and I shall have more to say about the substance of their ideological positions as we continue.

My third question is the *question of alienation*. One of the dominant themes in intellectual circles today is that of alienation. With its best known introduction in the sociological writings of Marx, Durkheim, and Weber, its problems are by no means new. That concern with alienation has again become fashionable is a matter of record; but that such concern should crop up in all three papers suggests to me that it is worthy of some consideration.

One of the major undercurrents of Drucker's essay, stemming from his concern with individual freedom, is his conviction that the diffusion of political power in society has led to a sense of *powerlessness* on the part of its members, and that such a sense of powerlessness is correlated with, if not in fact a cause of, other forms of alienation. Specifically, he addresses himself to the presumed loss of identity and autonomy. While Dahl does not go as far as Drucker, he too suggests that powerlessness, this sense of feeling alienated from the means of political control, is also a necessary concomitant of the diffusion of political power. Thus, Dahl suggests that those failing to participate in the decision-making process because their immediate goals did not appear to be involved, often develop a feeling of powerlessness when they later discover that they have to bear the consequences of decisions in which they took no part.* Miller, in contrast, does not give currency to the issue of powerlessness, but rather introduces another facet of alienation, namely *anomie,* or normlessness. The intriguing point here is that Miller in invoking anomie goes well beyond his colleagues in suggesting that the breakdown of the political structure of the community is in part a function of the breakdown of the normative structure of the community. Anomie, then, becomes his independent variable and the dispersion of political power his dependent variable.

My fourth question is a *question of power-arrangements in a democracy,* which I shall divide in two. The first I call the

* This point was not developed by Dahl in his paper. It emerged, rather, in a question and answer period following his talk when he spoke briefly about the "problem of consent" in a democratic society. Dahl distinguished several dimensions of consent. At one extreme, he suggested, are those people who are vague and uninformed about public policy and who do nothing about participating in the decision-making processes. At the other extreme are those who have very definite and concrete ideas about public policy and who participate a great deal. American society he characterized as being distinguished mainly by the former of these extremes — by passive consent and an extensive lack of participation. As Dahl states it, "[This] means that, by and large, the people who are most interested and most concerned about an area of policy are the ones who are most likely to be active in it. So one gets a system of policy-making in which the people . . . whose immediate interests are most heavily concerned are also the people who make the policy. This is a small minority of the total population. . . . [It] means one ends up with a very much larger portion of the population for whom consent, or in some cases dissent, is passive. Now the unfortunate consequence of this is that time and time again it means that people wake up and discover that the policies that were made by the people whose immediate and direct interests were involved have consequences for them that they dislike. . . . They may . . . be drawn into a kind of disgruntled feeling about the state of the system, that this system is run by people who don't pay any attention to people like me. That, it seems to me, helps give rise to this belief that there is a power-elite." Thus, we pay the consequences for our passive consent.

"problem of effective opposition." Clearly, one of the vital, yet unresolved, questions of political theory is that of the kind of resistance permissible in a democratic society. Does a national strike, a strike in a vital industry, or for that matter, a strike of public employees represent the illegitimate use of power? Drucker has suggested certain criteria of illegitimacy in his paper: discipline, organization, training, capability for mass action, and control of scarce resources. But certainly Miller's researches have demonstrated that for any group or coalition to exercise successful control it must possess these characteristics to some degree. How much and what kind of opposition can a democratic political system permit before the defeat or burgeoning of the opposition groups destroys the very system itself? Drucker, in a question period, dismissed the question of the criteria of illegitimacy, appealing to some core agreement or to some intuitive feelings about what constitutes legitimacy and illegitimacy. Since I do not share these intuitive feelings, I shall call upon him to make them explicit.

The second question I call the "problem of governmental domain." The problems of suburban sprawl, recognized by all of our panelists, confront us with the problem of what new political arrangements are necessary for coping with the changing economic and geographic bases of the metropolis. This problem, however, is but a small example of the continuing and, I suspect, increasing difficulty of the relationships that obtain, or ought to obtain, among all levels and units of government in a large-scale industrial society. Can we have both a strong central government and a strong local government as Drucker suggests? Does this question even make sense? Or can we reconstitute the power of the local community in accord with Miller's proposals? For that matter, can we operate at all within the existing political units and boundaries? I submit that the changes, the almost revolutionary developments in modern American society, challenge for the first time in this century our whole conception of democratic government. And if the members of the panel will forgive my raising such a basic issue, which, though I think this has been implicit in all of their presentations, I suggest that part of our dilemma is that we are no longer certain of the limits of governmental responsibility. Two consequences which have flowed from our uncertainty and ambivalence have been the growth of the fourth estate — that is, the shifting of political control to administrative agencies, and the increasing trend in local government not to initiate action but to act only after power mobilization has taken place in the community. This may be good politics, but it is certainly poor government.

My fifth question is the *question of the effectiveness of government*. It seems to me quite likely that many kinds of power-arrangements can operate compatibly within a democratic framework. Effectiveness is thus dependent upon one's personal model of power-arrangements. Whatever these models may be, it is obvious that the evaluation one places on the existing political structure depends also on how one perceives that structure. Dahl and Miller quite obviously do not share each other's observations about the nature of the existing power-structures, so that even if they shared the same model of power — which they do not — they would be forced into different evaluations of the effectiveness of the existing structures. For Miller, local government is a relatively weak power-center, dominated in most communities and on most issues by business, with the power of most other groups significantly neutralized and curtailed. For Dahl, political power, rather than being a constant, is relative to the issues at hand and different issues call forth different parties of interests. Few groups lack some political resource by which they may exercise some control.

My sixth question is a *question of methodology*. I am not going to touch the thorny and highly specialized question of how one locates and identifies those who hold and exercise power. This is an issue of limited concern. There is a prior and more fundamental methodological question — that of the social conditions that determine or give rise to different power-arrangements. Instead of simply going in and looking at the existing power-arrangements we should ask the prior question: What are the characteristics of communities or nations that give rise to given power-arrangements? Clearly, the answer here must be based on comparative research, on a model of experimentation. Historical research is necessary but not sufficient for such an experimental model. If Dahl wishes to use New Haven illustratively, it is all right, but this is not demonstration. Miller has been very much aware of this; in fact, in his book, *Industry, Labor and Community,* he makes a rather strong point of the need for comparative research. He has indeed attempted to do it; but I am not clear as to his reasons for attempting it as he did. Why choose Pacific City and English City? To what extent do these cities constitute a scientifically legitimate utilization of a comparative research design?

My seventh question is a *question of ethics,* the ethics of study. We are studying living people, living groups, living societies; and in studying them and eliciting their co-operation, we have certain ethical and moral responsibilities. What are the consequences for Pacific City, English City, New Haven, El Paso, Juarez, and the many other communities which have been and are now being studied? What are the consequences of the published reports we present them? Surely the question of power is a question within the public domain, but certainly there are going to be individual and societal consequences of such study. Surely, too, we must enter into some agreement with the people we study as to how we may report our findings. Let me give an illustration. An anonymous town called "Springdale" somewhere in New York State, was investigated by two rather ingenious political sociologists. The consequences of the publication of their book resulted in the authors being hung in effigy; their book was paraded down Main Street atop a hay wagon loaded with horse manure. The real issue was the failure of the researchers to inform the community as to how they intended to utilize their research findings. The members of the community

97

were highly embarrassed by the negative picture painted of them in the research report.

Finally, I raise the *question of justice*. I think that few will argue with Drucker that justice cannot be responsibly dispensed by administrative agencies and that it is increasingly being done. Certainly we are reaching the crisis stage with respect to the structure of our judicial and law enforcement institutions. The structure of our courts is inadequate for our present needs, and the growing web of unsystematically developed, vague, ambiguous laws has further enmeshed our judiciary in debate and delay. Our police systems have grown, duplicated, become more efficient and more effective. Professional schools of police administration have appeared. At the same time their growth and duplication is alarming. In 1950, the best estimate I could find showed 40,000 separate and distinct police agencies in the United States (one of the largest of these being an arm of an administrative agency, the New York Port Authority). Unfortunately, the growth of police, the ambiguity and changing character of law, delay and breakdown of judicial process, and the no longer clear distinction in contemporary society between the observers and the violators of law, present us with fundamental problems. Drucker asserts that there is some necessary and essential relationship between the judiciary and the persistence of democratic government. This is of course the case, but surely we must confront the *nature* of this relationship, and here, given time, I shall present this question to our panel.

As a matter of procedure, we shall begin again on my questions now that they have been stated. I should like to start with Professor Miller on the question of conceptualizing power. I accused Miller of not taking into consideration, or at least of not demonstrating that he took into consideration, the issue of power as potential and the relationship between potential power and its exercise.

Miller — This question brings to the fore the principal controversy over the method in which we shall try to identify community power. There are three distinct ways in which one can look for power in a community setting. One can look for potential power-offices, that is to say, for the heads of the largest manufacturing plants, the heads of the large banks, the heads of the largest mercantile establishments, the superintendent of schools, the heads of the largest church agencies of the biggest churches in town, and others in that category. This kind of search for potential power-offices represents one possible approach. I have made out a schedule of such power-offices, as have a few other researchers. We can affix the names of the people who occupy those offices, and we can say that here are the people who speak for the major institutional sectors of the community. Therefore, they surely must be the power-holders of this community, the people that are most influential in initiating and sanctioning policy.

A second method is to inquire among knowledgeable people whom they believe to hold power. It is probably best to ask so-called Top Influentials whom they consider to be the most powerful among them. Whether the city is a city of a half million or thirty thousand, it is almost equally possible to find ten, twelve, or fifteen people whom the entire community nominates over and over again as the people possessing the most influence. They have the reputation of power. How did they get it? People judge differently, of course. They see people active in community life. Most of those nominated belong, in a place like Pacific City, to an average of fifteen different organizations. They are directors in investment houses, in banks; they are in almost all the important social organizations; they are active in civic organizations; they are active in community projects.

A third method consists in following issues. This means, of course, that one can try to follow the chain of individuals who are taking part in the development of an upcoming issue. Some researchers have followed issues after they have been resolved, i.e., in retrospective investigation. I was asked how I view power.

In fact I've been accused of not viewing power as potential. Quite the opposite is true: The main method on which I have relied has been the reputational-associational method. This involves identifying those people who are believed to be most influential. Persons nominated as influentials are asked the question: If you were the chairman of a committee which was to make policy, or at least to gather advice for a leading policymaker, and if you wanted to get the fullest support of the community, what people would you nominate on the committee? We asked that of businessmen, of churchmen, of educators, or anyone who is acknowledged to be influential in the community. The answers which come forth identify a set of Key Influentials or Top Influentials. Now this is power-potential and it is precisely what I have tried to do. I have not used the list of potential officeholders, because studies made between those nominated by repute and those simply occurring as the chief holders of office show that the correlation is quite low, maybe a 50 per cent overlap. At least half of those potential officeholders do not attain nomination on the basis of their reputation for power. The reason they do not is because the only avenue to power open to those seeking it is activity. Activity is essential. The aspirant to power must be present in the arenas of community decision-making; he must stand up and be counted on isues or projects or at least he must be seen and noted. There are many people who hold potential-power positions who do not function; they are simply not active, they withdraw — and the withdrawers tend to be in the religious sector, in the educational sector, in the mass communications sector. The ones who are really active tend to be in the business and in the labor sector. So I would say that I have been very much concerned with power as a potential, and I think it is the quickest and most effective way to get the pattern for a community.

The leaders of repute are people who have been known over a lifetime of action; they have been watched over many, many issues; and, as a matter of fact, these leaders in Pacific City and

English City are people who on the average have lived 20 to 25 years in these communities. Now, simply to examine a given issue that is currently running only takes a little slice out of the power-structure. By the way, it is very difficult to follow such an issue. One can be very easily misled. Not much of a pattern emerges, because the only way to get a pattern for a community is to watch a whole series of issues, which takes a very long time. I know of no researcher who has done what he ought to do if he takes the issue approach. This, of course, is the approach of active power. I do not think that it is as effective for the researcher as the reputational method.

Ehrlich — I know, Professor Dahl, that you have some comments on this. When you are addressing yourself to the question of issues, I hope you will tell us how you came to choose the issues you did and, perhaps, why you think that these issues are representative of all the issues which confront the community.

Dahl — The problem that has always bothered me about the reputational method is its latent circularity. Miller says that he gets a group of influentials who then nominate Key Influentials. How do you know whether they are influentials? What is the test of it? Do you ask of other people whether they are influential, and how do you test the projections of these other people? This could go on *ad infinitum*. I do not see it as an objective test by which we know whether the people who finally get on his list are influential or not. Speaking rigorously, all we could say would be that Miller has a list of people who have reputations for influence — and we would never say anything more than that, for, this is actually all we know. If I were to be rigorous in my use of language about my people, I would say that I have a list of people who have initiated or vetoed alternatives with respect to these domains, or these scopes, over this period of time. I would not say anything more. There might be a great deal of growth in precision if we would stop talking about power and influence, and instead use the exact operational language that specifies what we did. Then, too, what has also worried me about the reputational approach is not inherent to it, but seems to be a characteristic of its actual use. It is the failure to ask the key questions in such a way as to discover if it is true that people who are influential in one area are not influential in another. Now it may be that this is not the case, but questions ought certainly to be so designed that if it is the case the question would enable one to find out. I am persuaded that if the question is phrased in the general way in which Miller has asked his questions, it would be impossible to find out even if power were specialized by sector. I think we ought also to be very rigorous about the whole problem of power-potential. It is easier to be rigorous conceptually, I may say, than it is in research. Ehrlich has asked a very penetrating question that goes to the heart of the whole problem. What do we mean when we say that somebody has the potential to influence somebody else, or that a group has the potential to influence somebody else? This is evidently different from saying that this person or this group has won on an issue, or that this is a particular issue on which the person or group did so and so. What conditions do we have to specify in order to be rigorously precise in meaning? It seems to me that we have to specify, first of all, the group, category, or class of persons. We have to specify the group of people we are talking about — whether they are businessmen, labor leaders or something else. Next, we have to specify what resources we expect the members of this category to have at their disposal. If we are talking about businessmen, can we make some estimate of what sort of political resources they have at their disposal? Third, we have to make a further statement as to the level at which we expect the members of this category to use their resources under these circumstances. It doesn't mean much to say, for example, that the power-potential of businessmen is higher than labor's unless we specify that businessmen are going to use their resources at maximum, or half of maximum — for instance, use all the money they have for politics, or use half the money they have. The statement without a reference to the level of resource use isn't meaningless, but it is very inexact. In the next place we have to specify something, even if only in a very general sort of way, as to what we expect their level of political skill is. Do these men really know what they are doing, or are they blundering idiots in the field of politics? If they lack skill, it may not matter if they spend a million dollars. Then we have to ask another question: What do we expect to be the degree of co-operation or unity among them? If the people in our category — businessmen, say — are all using their resources at a very high level of skill, but if they are using these resources in opposition to one another, then we would expect certain consequences to follow that would be different from what these would be if they were using their resources in co-operation. Finally, if we want to be rigorous about this, we not only have to specify what we expect to happen under all of these conditions but we have to specify the state of resource use and its skill, and the combination in all of the other significant sectors of the community. We can't simply say that the businessman under such and such circumstances is going to be powerful, unless we specify what it is the laboring people are doing, or what it is the average voter is doing, or what the small businessman is doing, or what half a dozen other kinds of groups in the community are doing. Now, what I say is this: Depending upon the conditions which you specify, you can point to any group in the community and say that it is potentially a dominant group in the community. There are no absolutely unreasonable conditions that would make it impossible to contend that any numerous group, under certain circumstances in the use of its resources and skills, wouldn't be a dominant group in the community. But we cannot, I'm saying, make any sort of general prediction about what is likely to happen unless we are basing it on past experience. I know of no other way of deriving a prediction about the future that isn't simply working out of a theoretical model. As I was saying a moment ago, we can have different theoretical workings-out of this problem depending on the conditions specified, but if we want to draw on experience then we have to draw on what has happened in the past in the community. It seems to me that on this ground Miller's conception of potential and my conception of potential are very different. I'm aware of the fact that many people have a strong concept of the power-potential of various groups in the community — the businessman, the Masons, the Catholic Church, or the Negro, or any one of a dozen groups — but it is critically necessary if they want to talk about their potential, that they specify all of the conditions that I have named, not only with respect to the one group but also with respect to the conditions that are likely to pertain to all of the other groups in the community.

Ehrlich — In taking issues, in part, as your focus, how is it that you select your issues, and what evidence can you muster to the effect that these issues truly represent the universe of issues that confront communities?

Dahl — I don't think it is possible to specify the universe of issues in a community with any great degree of exactness. We don't really know what this universe is. However, we can do something like this: We can take some sectors about which there would be little dissent — if anybody were asked — regarding their importance over the last few years. In the case of New Haven we chose public schools because they take, year in and year out, the largest amount out of the city budget. We took urban redevelopment because so much had been happening in New Haven. We took political nominations because it seemed to us that it was important to know how people got into office. On the other hand, there were some important areas which we neglected, and I regret that we did neglect them. We neglected the Community Chest, and we didn't do very much about welfare decisions. Then in the middle of our research, a charter proposal was turned down. It was perfectly clear to us that we had to know why this was turned down, so we reconstructed that decision in great detail. There is, then, a certain arbitrary element in this selection. Ideally, what one would like to say either is that he has chosen all the aspects in which the government acts or he has, in some sense, chosen a representative sample. Since it is very difficult to know what is meant here by a representative sample, one ought ideally to choose all of them. This is impossible, however, because time is lacking. Once these sectors have been specified, however, all that can really be said at the end of the research is that in these sectors this is the pattern of influence found. By the choosing of several different sectors, if it is found that influence is specialized with respect to these different sectors, at least it becomes clear, even if nothing else is known, that there isn't a single homogeneous power-elite. In order to test the hypothesis that there is a single homogeneous power-elite, it doesn't much matter *what* is chosen as long as long as three or four *different* sectors are chosen and concentrated on. Once the sector to be examined has been selected, it is no longer so difficult to choose the specific issues or decisions in a somewhat nonarbitrary but not entirely defensible way. Then the people who participated in a specific issue or decision in a fairly salient way are asked: What do you people regard as the most important things that have happened, or the most important issues that you have engaged in, in the last decade? Perhaps about ten major issues in each sector will be found which can then be followed through — partly with documents, but mainly by interviewing and reconstructing from the people who participated. The next question to be answered is, what sort of people were the most influential in these issues — in the sense that, from the historical record, they are found to have been relatively successful in initiating or vetoing policy proposals.

Miller — I'd like to comment on that. Professor Dahl said today if a study of issues led to a designation of the same influence-leaders as one got through the reputational method, then obviously we were talking not about different power-structures but the same power-structure. Now I am not opposed to the issue approach. As a matter of fact, practically all researchers have combined the reputational and issue approach. Floyd Hunter did this in Regional City; he did this in Salem, Massachusetts; he did this in his study of top leadership. I, too, sought in any way I could the issues with which the Key Influentials had been associated. There is one thing, though, I think we can be misled about. Dahl has just spoken about finding a number of issues in different sectors, because he's got that concept in his head. Now, my concept is different. What I would like to find is the issue that shakes the community from top to bottom. I found just one in my lifetime, the "right-to-work" petition in the State of Washington. In this kind of issue most of the leaders in major institutional sectors took a stand. The Catholic Church said this was a moral issue and opposed a right-to-work amendment. The Democratic party came out blatantly and strongly against it, and of course the labor unions stood shoulder to shoulder in opposition to it. And opposed to them were the business groups of the community, the largest business groups as well as some of the small industrial and mercantile groups. In this instance you see the power-structure now because it's revealed. What is revealed? The Key Influentials, the community organizations and associations which take stands, and some of the resources that can be marshalled. I am concerned that Professor Dahl may be deceived by a spatter of nonsalient issues which cannot display the true structure of community power. He may not be identifying the Top Influentials. When you have an issue it may very well be that in the initial stage the question of who will serve on the committee will come before the upper-limits people. They may say: Well, let's have the dirty work done, the leg work done, by lower-limits or understructure personnel. The mayor may appoint some of these. Very often the president of the Chamber of Commerce, the presidents of Rotary and Kiwanis, are "comers." They are understructure; "their heads are up." They're active, their names are in the paper but they are not really upper-limits people. You can follow issues, but if these issues are carried by understructure or lower-limits people, you may be misled. They're just understructure, and though they're out there doing the leg work, they may not have the sanction of the upper-limits people. What you've got to do is to have an issue that agitates this entire structure so the real influentials appear. They must take stands. It's known that they are in this thing: They have contributed money, they make a statement in the paper, they're seen together on a committee which is discussing this thing. Then you know that this group is on hand. Issues must be sanctioned, must be initiated, must win the support eventually of the upper-limits personnel.

Drucker — I hope it is permissible for a nonsociologist to say that he will not accept the term "influentials," does not believe in it, and that all our experience has indicated that there is no such animal. I submit that this concept of the "influentials" is a completely misunderstood and mistaken analogy taken from early anthropological study of some primitive tribes which had only one culture. Any more developed society has a multitude of cultures and in each culture you have entirely different decision-makers and entirely different decisions to handle. The real nub of the political process is, what culture is relevant? Where does this issue belong? That determines who has the standing on it, not the other way around. Then, as an old politician, I must say I'm surprised at the lack of recognition that what issues are important and what issues are relevant is very largely a result of individual personalities. There is such a thing as leadership, and it makes a difference. Don't compare Pacific City which has never in its life known any leadership, as an overgrown lumber camp, with what is the oldest, next to Venice, maritime oligarchy in the world, namely English City, which has an unbroken history of being a merchant city from before Roman times. There you are comparing a situation in which one individual can make a tremendous impact, because society is still exceedingly unformed, with a completely stylized situation where the only impact an individual can make is by moving away from it. You can't compare the two. Personalities and history do make a difference, and of the two personality makes a greater difference.

Ehrlich — I shall turn this next question first to our political theorist. What seems to you to be the differences in the ideological focus that characterize the panel, and perhaps even those political sociologists who are sociologists and those who are political scientists?

Dahl — Let me say that I am glad that I have been readmitted to the political science fraternity. I have been read out of the political science profession by many people, and twice at least today by my honored colleague, Drucker.

On the question of ideological focus, I'm not sure that the ideological differences are perhaps as sharp as your comments are implying. There is a difference, though I'm not sure that it is ideological as much as it is a difference in conceptions of the key characteristics of society that comes about from differences in training and in the kind of things we are accustomed to read and to look at. I think the sort of people who have been looking at communities in my way are predisposed to believe that American society is pluralistic and lacking in tightly integrated centers. I think the people who look at it in Miller's way are predisposed quite the other way: They do expect to find an integrated center somewhere. Secondly, we pluralists are more likely to assume that ordinarily in an American community there isn't a great deal of conflict and cleavage, that communities are more consensual in character than they are divided. These are empirical questions, however, and the only way we can establish the facts is by asking the right questions.

Miller has suggested that the kind of issue you want to look at is one that divides the community, that splits it wide open. All right—I agree. One wants to look at that kind of issue, if it occurs. Ordinarily it doesn't occur. If it occurred very often, we wouldn't have any political society. The political society would be destroyed; so most of the time what you are talking about presumably is not that kind of issue. Miller found only one, but I think that when that kind of issue is found it must be followed through to see what happens. Surely such issues would nicely test Miller's theory, for it must inevitably be the case, I would assume from his analysis, that right-to-work proposals passed in every state and were never defeated by the labor movement. That is to say, if it were true that this combination of business-men and wealth was dominant in most communities, and if its interests were most heavily involved in so-called right-to-work legislation, then everywhere these proposals should have passed. All that I am saying is this — I think that this isn't the case; it sometimes happens that one side may win, but sometimes the other side wins. There are conditions under which the other side, the opponents of so-called right-to-work laws, does win. Now one reason — and Miller's theory doesn't take it into ac-count — is the possibility that there are costs to being influential. It is not costless to exercise your influence. If we have a strong desire to maintain our influence in one sector, it may be that we will always concentrate our resources in that sector, knowing that it is just too costly to get involved in another. But the same may be true of the people who dominate the second sector, that they consistently dominate it, knowing that it would be too costly to try to dominate the first sector. Why too costly? They may lose their reputations; they may seem to be acting in a sec-tor where their views lack legitimacy. Businessmen, as far as I can tell from looking at my one and possibly atypical com-munity, have a certain legitimacy when they talk about certain kinds of problems and act within certain sectors, but once they get outside of them they no longer retain this acceptability. P.T.A. chairmen and superintendents of schools have a lot of legitimacy when they act in some areas, but if they get in others such as redevelopment, suddenly their influence, their persuasive-ness, and their political legitimacy decline. Or again, there are certain kinds of experts who will be accepted in one area but they won't be accepted in another.

To sum up, I don't see how Miller can have it both ways. He implies that the issues on which his power-elite isn't dominant are simply trivial or, as he puts it, "a spatter of nonsalient issues." Hence, the members of his power-elite don't get out and fight; if they did, he implies, then of course they would be dominant — which I take to mean they would win. There are other issues, Miller says, that shake the community from top to bottom; these are issues his power-elite really does regard as important. If so, then these should furnish a good test of his theory, for if his hypothetical power-elite doesn't pretty regularly win on these issues, it simply isn't dominant. Well, does it win on these issues or doesn't it? This is why I keep returning to the example of the New Deal: Did his power-elite win or lose — or was the New Deal also a "spatter of nonsalient issues"? Or take his own example: Has his hypothetical power-elite regularly succeeded in getting so-called right-to-work proposals passed? If not, how can we account for these defeats within the framework of Miller's theory? I don't know what happened in the State of Washington, which Miller cites, but I should think the outcome would be highly relevant to his theory. Did his power-elite win or lose? I do know that while right-to-work proposals passed in some states — generally with the support of farmers, who present an interesting problem for Miller's analysis — in others, particularly some of the most highly industrialized states, these proposals were defeated. How do these defeats square with Miller's theory? If businessmen aren't dominant on some issues because these are issues they don't care about, and if they get defeated on some of the most important issues they *do* care about, then in heaven's name how can they be called "dominant"? Influential, yes; but dominant, no.

Miller — I've been saddled with a misconception here. It's been said that sociologists who enter the study of power come out with monolithic pyramids of power and that political scientists seem to come out with pluralistic conceptions of power. I do not believe this to be true. As a matter of fact, I have tried to show very clearly that English City does not have a monolithic pyramid of power. You must remember that research in this area is very new and not very extensive. Most of us, of course, are talking out of the background of our own research experiences and because of this we can only study a few cities, even in a lifetime. Therefore, we really do not know whether we have the full spectrum of the range of variety in American cities, let alone the cities of the world. I think, though, we do have a conception of the fact that cities vary in many different respects. One of them is in the nature of power. I want to talk of, now, not one, not two, but five different power types. The first is the one we see on the cowboy shows, the baron who dominates the cow town; or perhaps this is the industrialist in the one-company-dominated town: Mr. Big with his lieutenants, where each person in line is beholden to him for his job, and where his approval must be won for anything of importance. That's our *pyramid based on one person*. Now in multi-industry towns, where of course the power is divided between the powerful business groups, we can find a little aristocracy. In Middletown, Mr. Ball not only produced the Mason Jars, but he produced sons, and his sons had businesses, and the Ball people now had a little aristocracy there. And it was to them that the rest of the community was beholden. *A pyramid based on aristocracy,* then, is our second type. Then there is the pyramid that was found in the South in Regional City, with its four distinct layers. The first, a group of top industrial, manufacturing, financial, and mercantile people. Then comes the second layer: vice presidents, general managers, and the top civic personnel. Then your news commentators, your petty civic officials, and the like; and down below are the fourth-raters: teachers, ministers, and welfare workers. I found that this *stratified pyramid* was approximated in Pacific City but not entirely. Fourth is English City, a *ring structure,* a whole set of power structures which come to convergence. There's a first-rate group here composed of many different institutional sectors: the president of the university, the head of the Labour party, the bishop of the Episcopalian church, a duke from the society sector. Then we can see a kind of second-rate group, and you can even identify a third-rate group. What is important here is that it is ringed; that is, at the top are representatives of all the major institutional sectors. Finally, Professor Dahl seems to have found a community which has *segmented pyramids.* In other words, there is an educational power-pyramid, there is a business power-pyramid, a religious power-pyramid, and so on. Whatever the issue is, if it galvanizes the people that are concerned with that type of issue, a special power-pyramid is created. I have no doubt that all of these power structures exist and unless the total range of them is grasped we can not begin to think clearly and concisely about power.

Now, I want to answer only one more question and lay this to rest. I've heard it twice now. If the business group dominates in the community, and if the businessmen are Republican, why don't the Republicans win every election? The reason they don't win every election is because there are latent power-sectors, and when those latent power sectors are galvanized they can come to bear in elections. Those are often the little people who are never admitted or who never try to influence the political life of the community. These are the people who are indifferent. One never knows whether they'll get up enough gumption to go to the polls on Election Day, but these are the people who, once excited enough about a political campaign, come out and vote. These potential sectors can always be galvanized, and the largest group in a community is certainly the nonbusiness interests. I have emphasized the point that in American communities there is no formal legitimate center of power. The city council is weak, local government is mushy, the power-centers are in the Chamber of Commerce, in the central labor union, in the political parties, in the council of the churches, in the P.T.A., and in the American

Legion. This is where issues are debated, this where power is generated, and this is where pressure is then put on the council to sanction what these independent power-groups have carried out. And the point is that after election, after all the shouting has died away, who is back on the scene? Back on the scene are the Key Influentials, predominantly of business influence, who day by day are active in considering the policy matters that affect their business and their community. They are the ones who make the key decisions on the issues which arise and are not submitted to electoral referendum. It is for that reason that they are significant, and it is for that reason that Republicans do not always win elections.

Ehrlich — Let us indeed lay this to rest. Let us turn our discussion now to the problem of alienation. We have the agreement between Dahl and Drucker on the growing sense of powerlessness, and the feeling, I think, on the part of Dahl that perhaps this sense of powerlessness is one of the fundamental dilemmas of contemporary society. Drucker goes way beyond this into a personal anxiety, if you will, that powerlessness ultimately leads to some form of self-alienation. Miller, in contrast, suggests that normlessness, the breakdown of the normative structure of the community, and the feeling of normlessness on the part of individuals has led to the diffusion of power. Dahl countered by suggesting that the local community never possessed solidarity and that normlessness cannot be construed as the antecedent of the diffusion of power.

Miller — I think this is an extremely tough question. Is the cement falling out of society, especially local community society? I can only say that an overwhelming group of observers answers this affirmatively, and that our communities are not the established societies of old. We don't put our roots down in them. Every semester, I ask my university class in social problems, which is composed of about sixty students, the question: "How many of you plan to go back to your home community to live and work there?" I am always surprised if I see four or five hands go up. Out of that sixty, fifty-five, right now, are committed not to go back to live and work in their home community. What's more, wherever they're going, they're going to move several more times. And the four or five are going to be deceived because I don't think they will remain in their home communities all of their lives. We are a society on the move. We put down roots because a job exists. If a better job opportunity arises we go to that job, and everything else has to take second place. We leave our parents, we leave the home town, we leave our friends, we cut all ties for the good job, and everybody gives moral sanction to that. "Yes, son, yes you should go where your best opportunity is." And so we go. Corporate life of course has only encouraged that. Now, this is a serious problem. We've got to put down roots; we've got to know people, we've got to know political candidates — it takes time to know a community. I feel I know English City better than any community I ever lived in, because I seriously and systematically studied it for one year. I've never done that to a community in which I've lived. The problem in terms of influentials is this: You do not get nominated as a Top Influential unless you are identified as a person stable in that community. What that meant in English City and in Pacific City is that one had to live there from 20 to 25 years. Most of the leaders were born there. It doesn't do any good to be the top-notch military dog, to be the naval commander in Pacific City for example, because everybody knows the Navy will move him sooner or later. It's no good to be a corporate manager if people know that a better job, higher up in the hierarchy in some other community, is beckoning him. He is not regarded as a real community settler. And thus, all people on the move are partially alienated. Now another form of alienation that disturbs me is the neutralization of certain sectors. For example, I think educators, religious leaders, civil servants, welfare workers — all of these people are increasingly neutralized. There are many reasons for it. They're on salary, they've got to watch their p's and q's.

114

They play it safe. Corporations tell their people, "Now, don't upset the boat." This curtails political activity and alienates the person from citizenship. Among professionals, where one would expect a high order of civic leadership, we are finding a pattern of almost total work absorption. It's a curious society where some people are working less and less and others are working more and more. There is no end to the demands on the professional. He could work day and night and he couldn't read all the literature in his field. I asked various lawyers why they weren't more active, and they said they just simply could not pull away from their offices — work was too demanding for civic participation. Doctors find it almost impossible to participate because of the great demands upon their professional time and efforts. This is alienating and neutralizing. Now these are the things that I see as alienation influences.

Drucker — Well, I should start out by saying that I am the one non-Thomist in this crowd, and therefore at a decided disadvantage even on semantics. My master has always been St. Bonaventure [simply because I don't have to pretend I understand him]. This leads to very different views, such, for instance, that I can't go along with Mr. Miller that research in communities is very new. It is very old and very extensive, only it was always practiced in the novel. If I want to know about communities, I still go to the novelist. The social scientists have not yet reached anything like the insight, the understanding of the community that the great novelists have.

As to Ehrlich's concern with the social responsibility of the researcher, I don't think Chaucer or Balzac were terribly worried about the impact of their research on their respective communities. And as to the Springdale story—thank God, there is still some literary criticism around which is not the new criticism but the old one.

I have a feeling that had Miller's predecessor a hundred years ago at the University of Indiana asked his boys there how many expected to go back to their home communities, he would not have had even four hands. Surely, a hundred years ago when a person went to college it was quite clear that he wasn't going to go back; to get away was the only reason he went to college. I am not convinced that the small community was such a happy place. I happen to have lived in small communities a good deal of my life, including one in New England that was as untouched by modern society in those years as it could be. I would not describe it as anywhere near a social utopia. As a matter of fact, it was an infinitely less harmonious, an infinitely more alienated, and infinitely more fear-ridden community than anything anyone could find, even in the Detroit jungle.

Let me say a few words about alienation. First, I am a little concerned that you consider it primarily, or even exclusively, as a social phenomenon. I think that it is an existential phenomenon of man. To look for its causes or its cure exclusively in society strikes me as being just a misunderstanding. The great analyst of of alienation was Kierkegaard, and he did not look for its causes in society, but in the basic impossibility of human existence.

Now as to the alienation of this modern society, I have wondered whether we can be as, shall we say, sweeping as Mr. Ehrlich described me as being. There is a problem, and it is not an American problem. Everything we have said so far applies to Japan and to South America, the two parts of the world that I know fully as well as this country. So we are talking of modern society. I think the characteristics of modern society are that relationships are made. It is not as our predecessors of one hundred years ago, the fathers of sociology, believed—a contract society. We have learned that there is no such thing. It is not possible. Society has to be a status society; but status used to be given. When Mr. Miller described English City, he described the English City of 100 years ago, not the English City of today. Yet it is the right description because English City still sees itself as it was 100 years ago when status was given; whereas today, even in English City, status has to be made, relationships have to

116

be established. I think this is the great change.

We might say our predecessors, our grandparents, who had more faith in the world than we have, would have hailed this as a great victory. We are often scared of it, and rightly so. It puts too much pressure on the individual who does not necessarily want to have to make such decisions. But this seems to me the essential difference: We are not automatically geared in a certain way. We have to gear ourselves in, which means, too, the option to opt out — to be not geared in at all. Nothing is simpler than to be outside of the community today, and there are many people to whom this is a great boon and a great enrichment of the personality. So this is actually what has really happened; it isn't alienation from society. It is that you have to determine yourself very largely what the relationships ought to be, can be, and should be.

This is frightening, this is not to everybody's taste, but I don't think that it is alienation. I think what it essentially is is that we have a status society, in which the status is not given but depends very heavily on what the individual makes of it. This may create tension and despair. But we know that other kinds of society produce as many pathologies as does our present one.

Dahl — I want to make sure that I am not really being held responsible for something that I may not have said, because my position is that I really don't know whether there has been an increase in a sense of alienation, for two reasons: first, I don't really know what the term means in any precise way, and second, I don't know of any persuasive data, information, or finding one way or another; therefore, I would like to keep open-minded and skeptical. I am, however, not the least bit persuaded by the rather large and grandiose theories on this subject, many of which were propounded by European theorists, some by Americans, but all of which, it seems to me, are based upon the scantiest kinds of evidence. I would just like to make one other point. I think it is easy to confound three rather different kinds of historical changes. One is the great historical transformation of medieval society into modern society. This had been going on for a long time, and I think there is no question that it has led to a good deal of rootlessness. But the post-medieval society has been with us now for a couple of hundred years. Surely, this isn't the question at issue. American society is entirely post-medieval. Yet here again there are two important distinctions. One is the impact of the industrial, commercial society upon old communities like New Haven, Boston, New York, Philadelphia, or Baltimore, which were previously hierarchical and stratified. The other was the incursion of commercial industry on essentially small western and middle-western agrarian communities. Obviously these are three different things, and the effects are all different. When de Tocqueville was here he made remarks which, if he had used the term alienation, would sound very contemporary — that we were a people who had no roots, that everybody was on the move, that nobody had a sense of identification with his community. Sixty years later Bryce wrote a book which was a kind of re-doing of de Tocqueville, and he made the same charge; and now, today, we assert it again. All that I'd like to say is that I don't really know; maybe it's true, maybe it's increasing, maybe it's decreasing, maybe it's been a constant in American life for a century or more, and maybe somewhere somebody has some good trend data. If so I've never seen them, and therefore I would prefer to adopt the position of open-mindedness and skepticism.

Ehrlich — I think we have time for one more question. I suggested that we were no longer certain of the limits of governmental responsibility and that the growth of the fourth estate, of administrative agencies, and the increasing trend in local government *not* to initiate action were consequences of our uncertainty or ambivalence about the limits of governmental responsibility. I should like to throw this open to all members of the panel for their reaction.

Drucker — I think that two things have happened that have changed what in the early nineteenth century would have been called "the limits of the state." First, society has become completely monetized. This is very new; even in highly developed societies it has occurred only in the last hundred years at the most. This changes the whole meaning of property, which simply ceases to mean what it used to, namely the one thing government cannot possibly take away. It could expropriate an individual but it could not eliminate property. But, in a totally monetized society there is no property, in the old sense; and in a totally monetized economy, government is capable of doing what no government ever could do, namely, mobilize the total economic resources of the community for public purposes.

The second thing that has happened is military technology. It isn't so very long ago that an organized group with simple weapons at its command could defeat a highly organized professional army. It isn't so very long ago that the maximum of military technology that any society could possibly produce was equivalent to about 4 or 5 per cent of its national income, not because it couldn't raise more money, but because it couldn't raise more arms. There weren't enough skilled people capable of producing them. The explosive element in military technology which has, I think, undermined the modern state completely is its power, absolute power, and the capacity to destroy itself and others. This is simply not within the concepts of political power as we have known it. How you tame these two monsters is, I think, one of the essential problems that we have.

I am a pluralist to the extent of not only believing in conflict but in believing that conflict is the ultimate safeguard of liberty. Therefore, I do not hold that the only way that one can neutralize power is by counter-power. We have a political leviathan created by the economic monetization of capital and by a capacity for total mobilization and total destruction. This raises problems of control of power such as we've never had before, and which will, I think, require means we've never had be-

fore. I think that we shall need radical political experimentation
— radical in the sense that we have never done it before — to
maintain the basic values, the basic commitments, the basic
freedoms and, above all, the basic conviction of government as
an instrument of the governed and not the other way around.

Miller — I would just say one thing. It is now apparent that there
are two major power-centers in American life. One is based
upon the economic interests of property and represented by
businessmen and those who affiliate their interests with business.
The second center of power is the labor union. It is around the
labor union that an opposing political party can be organized.
It is this power-center which is capable of bringing together a
large body of people with resources and talents. It is the countervailing power in American life today. Professor Drucker has told
us there are dangers in power. There is of course danger in either
of these two powers becoming too strong, but it is healthy, I
think, and one of the great signs of the twentieth century, that
we do have an opposing power-center in labor organizations
Workers — not just manual workers but, increasingly, white
collar workers, technicians, and professionals — stand in opposition to the leviathan, whether it is government, corporations, universities, or the church.

Dahl — As I look about our society what I am most impressed
by, as many people are, is the extent to which we waste our resources on private purposes rather than public purposes. This is
a privately oriented society, despite tasks confronting us that
seem clearly to require a massive reallocation of resources to
public purposes of all kinds. There is hardly a sector of community activity that is not starved for resources. There is hardly
a way to spend a dollar in the community more efficiently, more
effectively — no matter how much corruption or graft there is,
no matter how much dishonesty or bureaucratic red tape there
is — than spending it for public purposes, rather than spending

it for many of the private purposes to which it now goes. I therefore feel that if the American dream and the dream of the good community are going to be achieved or at least approximated in the next half century, then this is going to require a very sizable reallocation of resources for public purposes. This does not, however, necessarily require any one single technique or public purpose. It doesn't necessarily mean that the instruments to execute the public purposes all have to be strictly governmental. In the attempt to build what I, and I imagine most of us, here, would regard as a desirable and healthy local community, I would not be so sanguine as Professor Miller is that the leadership we need will come from the ranks of the labor movement. Unfortunately the record of the labor movement has been, so far, one of neglect of the local community.

There is some hope that this is changing, but I see very little prospect in this country of a major political force centered around the trade union movement. On the contrary, if there is a shift of resources to public purposes in the next decade, or even the next fifty years, I think it is going to come about as a result of actions by all sorts of diverse groups; for example, by people who are concerned about the education of their children. And these people are not just workers. They are all sorts of people, they're middle-class people, professional people, the teachers themselves — they come from every stratum of the community. In any area — public health, welfare, education, redevelopment, planning — the people who are most interested in it may not be and usually aren't strongly identified with the trade unions. The way we are likely to get a reallocation of resources to public ends is not through large political movements that split the community wide open, but probably, as these things have happened in the past, by small groups of fairly dedicated people who are concerned about a particular sector of policy and who are willing to spend some of their time and some of their own resources in changing policy in their direction. If it isn't going to happen that way, then I don't think it is going to happen at all.

Drucker — May I enter a dissent? First, let me start with Mr. Dahl's "more resources for public purposes." That, I must say, isn't the problem. The problem is — what public purposes? We devote today about one third of our national income to public purposes; the Federal budget has remained static, but state and local budgets have exploded. About fifty cents out of every dollar of additional national income since World War II has gone into public purposes. I submit that we are unlikely to do better. The real question will be, what public purposes?

This is going to create entirely different power groups from those Mr. Miller sees. He, I think, generalizes from the experience of the last ten or fifteen years. Yet, I submit, all the evidence shows that these are very largely spent forces. The labor unions represent a rapidly shrinking segment of our population — and a very old one indeed. Moreover, labor shows no signs of being able to get hold of the new majority, the educated and professional worker — not the slightest glimmer. Management, the experience of the last eight years has made clear, has very limited constitutional powers; it will not be asked to contribute more. By its very nature management is focused on one specific function.

Altogether, these are not two distinct power groups any more. The realities of our international economic situation will force us within the next few years to lump those two together as the producer interest, and to impose the common need on both. They are not opposing groups — they are complements — and have to be treated as complementary the moment one looks at the nation from the outside. At the water's edge, there is no conflict between management and labor any more. If the overriding national interest is, as it's going to be, to remain competitive in a rapidly expanding world economy, then these two will be one interest.

I submit further that there are already definite signs that the new power groups, the ones for the next ten or fifteen years, are three entirely different ones. The first group is the *public administrators,* especially those in state and regional areas. This is where

122

the challenge of public policy is today. The second group is the *educators* on all levels; and the third, the *armed forces*. I submit that these are our emerging real power-structures. Forget about business and labor, they represent the spent forces of yesterday.

Conclusion. In the foregoing pages we have presented three distinctive viewpoints. In the concluding chapter we will re-capitulate what has been said, draw out the common elements, and examine their implications for contemporary society.

William V. D'Antonio, Assistant Professor of
Sociology at the University of Notre Dame,
formerly taught at Michigan State University.
He has engaged in extensive research in
Mexican and American border communities,
dealing with the interrelationships of
business and politics. He is the co-author
with William H. Form of a recently completed book on
Business and Politics in Two Border Cities.

DEMOCRACY IN AMERICA: RETROSPECT AND PROSPECT

William V. D'Antonio
Howard J. Ehrlich

> *I do not fear tomorrow,*
> *because I have seen yesterday and I love today.*
> — attributed to William Allen White

The problems, the ideas, the issues that have been raised in these pages are certainly not new; what we hope is new is the manner in which they have been presented. We have brought together men with divergent viewpoints on some of the vital problems of democracy in America. We turn our attention now to a summing up and appraisal of the major ideas which have been presented. We shall look first at the conceptions of democracy, power and freedom that underlie the preceding chapters.[1]

DEMOCRACY

As a dominant value in American society, democracy serves as a guide and a principle for behavior. Too often, however, it serves merely as the rationalization for our actions, so that the mere invocation of the word itself is presumed sufficient to justify our behavior. What has happened is that the *word* has become

---

[1] The stimulus for our discussion of democracy, power and freedom comes from many writers. We wish in particular to acknowledge our intellectual indebtedness to the following men, whose relevant works appear in the appended bibliography: Chester Barnard, Robert Bierstedt, Thomas I. Cook, John K. Galbraith, Hans Gerth, Herbert Goldhamer, William Kornhauser, Seymour M. Lipset, Charles P. Loomis, Robert M. MacIver, C. Wright Mills, Barrington Moore, Jr., Edward A. Shils, and Max Weber.

valued, a sacred symbol — a shibboleth — to be revered and cherished. Invested with the sacred, it is not subject to critical examination. As it is more and more invoked as a sacred but empty symbol, its use as guide and principle becomes inhibited. Eventually its true meaning, as with many of the key words in our society, fades and becomes obscure.

No explicit, clear-cut definition of democracy was given in the foregoing pages. We shall try to abstract from the papers and discussion of our contributors precisely what they mean, and to present, by these means, our own perspective.

It is clear that Miller believes that a necessary condition of democracy is the existence of effective opposition to the business-men whom he has found trying to control the local community. In seeking to find issues that rock the community, that ignite the maximum of political participation throughout all institutional sectors, Miller argued that it is only in such cases that we can determine if there is an effective opposition, and hence democracy. Did the businessmen win or lose? In the right-to-work legislative struggle in Washington the businessmen lost: effective opposition was brought to bear against them. But Miller is still worried, for in the mundane day-to-day affairs of the community he finds little effective opposition to the businessmen.

There is implied but never made explicit in Miller's argument that the oligarchic control which the businessmen enjoy over community affairs is obtained not directly by force, but by the broad dissemination of business values: what is good for business is good for the community. Little organized resistance to this perspective has been found. That there is a lack of broad participation by leaders representing various institutional sectors, and a domination instead by those with business values, is demonstrated by Miller in his lists of reputed Top and Key Influentials. Other recent studies show substantially the same results.[2]

[2] See for example, William H. Form and Warren L. Sauer,

Have we achieved democratic community life? Miller's verdict is that we have fallen far short of our goal. Moreover, if we are willing to assume, as does the sociologist Morris Janowitz, that "effective decision-making at the community level is the prerequisite for democratic procedures in larger political systems," then the community power studies of Miller and others have even more far-reaching implications than the context in which they were conducted.[3]

Dahl would agree that democracy includes within its meaning the idea of effective opposition. He first considers the several kinds of political resources that are available to citizens in American society, and then examines the extent to which they have been, and are, controlled by one or several groups.

For Dahl, equality of *access* to political resources represents a vital criterion of political democracy. He argues that in the past, political resources were distributed unequally, and that these inequalities were cumulative. Power went to those with wealth and prestige. But the mark of contemporary America is that these inequalities, while they still exist, are no longer cumulative, or at least less so. Access to one resource does not guarantee access to another.

The right of each citizen to only one vote in an election has become a great leveling factor, and makes effective opposition to wealth and prestige not only possible but probable. Still, the system is imperfect at best. As Dahl states, there is no free and open competition within political parties for leadership at even the local level; a very small number of persons decides who will be the candidates for leadership. Nor is there a widespread participa-

"Organized Labor's Image of Community Power Structure," *Social Forces*, May, 1960; William V. D'Antonio, William H. Form, Charles P. Loomis, and Eugene C. Erickson, "Institutional and Occupational Representation in Eleven Community Influence Systems," *American Sociological Review*, June, 1961.

[3] Morris Janowitz (ed.), *Community Political Systems* (Glencoe: Free Press, 1960), p. 17.

tion over issues. What has occurred, rather, in the absence of either active consent or dissent, has been a *passive* consent on the part of the majority. This has led to an emphasis on consensus rather than conflict, and through this to a deprecation of this essential ingredient of democracy. While this may have the peculiar advantage of lending stability to the system, it may also threaten the freedom of the individual in the long run by eliminating any opposition, and by leaving the individual with the feeling that the system of political decision-making is outside his control. Through failure to participate, large numbers of people may be and are disenfranchised, by default, from the realization of values and derived goals which are central to them.

Democracy requires widespread participation by the majority of the citizens. However, if there is too much participation by too many people on all issues, the stability of the system may itself be threatened by an intense fractionalization of interests. If there is too little participation, the danger exists that a united minority may acquire control. But if the number of persons and intensity of participation are problems, certainly the effectiveness of participation is even more problematic. If participation is to be effective, then choice among the available alternatives of political action must be rational in the sense of maximizing knowledge and of minimizing the consequences of error. Clearly, the increasing complexity of technology and social organization in all phases of human endeavor operate, and increasingly so, against this. Perhaps the widespread lack of participation reflects not apathy, but the failure of the citizenry to comprehend the issues under consideration. Here then lies the role of leadership in a democracy: to present the issues and alternatives of policy in such a way that the citizenry can participate effectively if it will, and such that it will be concerned to participate.

There is another aspect to the problem of equality. It inheres in the concept of equality itself. It seems to be a popular and contemporary notion that in a democracy everyone must, perforce, enjoy an equal amount of whatever political resources are available. Yet the variety of potential political resources within our society is almost unlimited, and such a demand is a sociological absurdity. Certainly every individual does not, nor, could enjoy equal power on every issue. However, as far as the vote is concerned this is, more or less, the case; and here the demand of equal power is a *sine qua non* of democracy.

What we need to insist on, beyond the vote, is an equality of access or opportunity to acquire political resources and, hence, power. Even here, as Dahl puts it, this will not guarantee the equality of power. It merely means, that we may all start out more or less even in the race for inequality. The important thing, however, is that such "achieved inequality" is recognized as legitimate in that we recognize and sanction the right of those who win this contest for political resources — assuming they have played the game according to the rules of free and open competition — to influence and control our behavior in prescribed ways and within prescribed limits.

American democracy and the laws developed to sustain it, Drucker contends, are still tied to the image of the small city-state. As a consequence, our laws and political-legal institutions are no longer adequate to cope with the super-metropolis and the bureaucratic organizations that interweave themselves among them. The specialization of function and complexity of knowledge required to run such bureaucracies as the Civil Service, the military, and the various administrative branches of the government tend to invest such complex organizations with almost complete autonomy. Control by the people through opposition and participation in the decision-making process becomes more and more highly circumscribed. It is equally clear that we can no more have complete public control than we can permit the complete autonomy of these institutions.

We have thus far spoken of the vital ingredients of the democratic process: effective opposition, the equality of access to political resources, the vote, free and open competition for leadership, the role of leaders in presenting issues, and the balance between autonomy and control of the power centers of society. We turn now to a different order of considerations.

The ultimate rationale for a democracy is that it alone, among the political systems which man has devised to govern himself, best protects the integrity of the individual. But bureaucratic organization, which on the one hand serves many interests of the large-scale industrial society more efficiently and more effectively than any other form of social organization yet contrived, also makes more problematic the protection of the individual.

A fundamental belief underlying the practice of democracy is that every individual is deserving of respect by the simple fact of his humanity. Respect on this level is not a matter of achievement. It is a fact of social existence, obtained as an automatic concomitant of participation in group life. It entails the corollary belief that the end of group participation is the welfare of the individual. Insofar as this involves the establishment of formal groups to achieve this end, it must always be remembered that such groups are merely instruments designed to achieve the common good, the maximum protection and development of the individual.

If respect for the individual is requisite, so too is respect for his beliefs and opinions; or, at the very least, his right to espouse and proclaim them. In fact, one test of democracy is the extent to which it can suffer and enjoy the extremist. This poses another of the challenging dilemmas for a democratic system: How much difference can it permit without endangering the system itself? Surely if one accepts the dictum of difference without division, then it must follow that individuals or groups who clearly advocate divisive acts are no longer subject to the rules of the game, and the people must decide how they will protect themselves from those individuals or groups. It is, unfortunately (or possibly fortunately), not always a simple matter to determine what constitutes a divisive act.

Every society, by the very fact of its existence, has built into it an extensive pattern of consensus, that is, a complex of values, beliefs, and sentiments which guide behavior and give the several human organizations their structures. Consensus is a fact of social life; it is democracy that is problematic. Democracy must be built upon and developed out of an original system of consensus, and is sustained, just as any society itself is sustained, through consensus about its fundamental or ultimate beliefs and values. Paradoxically, democracy is guaranteed and made secure by conflict, not over its basic premises, but over derived goals or over means to achieve these goals. Fundamental conflicts are almost always minimized. Perhaps this explains why democracy in America has been characterized mainly by passive consent — because for most people and for most issues there appears to be only a remote relevance to democracy per se. Perhaps, too, this is why men like Miller seek the key issue that shakes the entire community. It is a key issue precisely because it is a quite direct challenge to ultimate values and beliefs, as well as to immediate goals. And certainly, Dahl is right in asserting that democracy is threatened by too much of this kind of conflict. Open conflict on too many issues at the same time poses a great threat to the system.

The problem of conflict is heightened by its context in a pluralistic society.[4] In such a society, almost by definition, there is no clear-cut hierarchically ordered system of values and beliefs. The problem for a democratic system in a pluralistic society is to reconcile the beliefs and values upon which it is based with those which constitute the consensual pattern of community life which are not necessarily essential to the maintenance of the democratic system, and in fact may be inimical to it.

In talking about democracy, we have here confined our discussion to that of a political democracy, only because this is the boundary of our assignment. Certainly we may talk of demo-

[4]   See John Courtney Murray, S.J., *We Hold These Truths* (New York: Sheed and Ward, 1960).

cracy within any social system — the family, school, office, church, and so on. Perhaps a crucial difference among political theorists who are also democrats is the degree to which they regard democracy as necessary beyond political government.

POWER

The problems of the usage of the concept of power and its derivatives in political sociology are far too numerous and complex to be accorded full treatment here. Our discussion, then, should be taken as orientative rather than exhaustive. Power in its most general sense refers to a capacity or ability to control others and, in this context, to control the decision-making process (which implies the control of others). We may focus upon power as a potential for control or through its exercise as control itself. These perspectives are, of course, not mutually exclusive. Persons who exercise power must, by definition, have had a power-potential; but not all persons who hold potential power do in fact exercise power.

This is the source of the Miller-Dahl controversy. Dahl with his focus upon issues is concerned with the exercise of power; Miller with his focus upon reputation is concerned with potential power. It is thus hardly surprising that they arrive at different depictions of the community power-structure. All other things being equal, their differences in findings are a function of their different research strategies, and their findings are — within the limits of these strategies — equally valid. We shall return to these findings later.

The two major components of power are *authority* and *influence*.[5] (A third component, *coercion,* which we will not be

[5] For a look at the variety of ways in which power has been treated, in the sociological literature, see among others: Charles P. Loomis, *Social Systems* (Princeton, N.J.: D. Van Nostrand Co., 1960), and the papers by Weber, Goldhamer and Shils, Barnard, Bierstedt, and Gerth and Mills, which appear in Lewis A. Coser and Bernard Rosenberg (eds.), *Sociological Theory* (New York: Macmillan, 1957).

concerned with here, has reference to that extreme form of control which is based on force or the threat of force.) Authority refers to the right to control the decision-making process in prescribed areas and under specified conditions. Authority resides in a position within an organized group; it is the position which is invested with authority, not the individual — who can exercise authority only as long as he occupies the position. The right to exercise authority is grounded in group norms, and legitimized by the fact that those with authority can be held accountable to the group for their actions and decisions.

Authority is a group phenomenon, a product of status relationships. Influence, by contrast, is an individual phenomenon, and a product of interpersonal relationships. Influence refers to control of the decision-making process on the basis of the personal qualities of the individual, e.g., popularity, reputation, skills in manipulating people, personal obligation, persuasiveness, and the like. The capacity to influence, then, resides in the individual and the facilities (skills and resources) at his disposal. In some measure, then, influence is a component of every social act.

There is invariably a constant interplay between authority and influence. While the obligation to obey the decision of a person in authority is limited, ideally in a very specific way, it must be recognized that the possessor of authority often has the opportunity to develop or increase his personal influence over the behavior of others. In fact it may be impossible for a person occupying a position of authority to avoid this, even if he wants to. The President of the United States may influence the behavior of millions even when there is no obligation to obey him. So also clergymen, scientists, labor leaders and others, speaking about problems which are outside the area of their authority, may influence others because their utterances are linked inevitably with their position. Such influence is not necessarily positive, of course. Indeed, the problem for the analyst is frequently that of isolating the components of power to determine the extent to which the exercise of power has occurred within the limits of democratic procedure. We shall now look in more detail at the way in which our contributors have handled the problem of power in a democracy.

Drucker's major concern is with the increased scope of political power and the greater diffusion of such power in the last fifty years and through all sectors of American society. Not only has the power of the government itself increased, other institutional sectors have become semi-autonomous power centers in their own right. What is disturbing to Drucker is that he sees these new centers of power as being without authority. They are accountable to no one and, as such, are almost uncontrolled and perhaps uncontrollable. If they have not yet acted irresponsibly — and on this point there could be much dispute — there is no guarantee that they will not. As such, the whole democratic process is threatened by their existence.

While for Drucker power has increased in all institutional sectors with government being merely the highest peak in a range of mountains, to Miller government as a source of power has declined relative to the business sector of the community. Miller contends that effective political power rests with businessmen, who are identified primarily as businessmen, but who exert predominant influence over the political decisions of the community. He further contends that the problem for the local community is to get these other sectors of power to participate, to become part of this mountain range of power.

There is agreement between Drucker and Miller to the extent that both question the authority of such institutional sectors to make decisions which affect the lives of many in the community. However, neither man clearly shows how the vested interests of any group are to be contained, so that power and authority are not falsely usurped. Both men see the need for new laws to make local government effective again, and both seek this achievement through dynamic leadership. Again, both men fail to confront the prior issue. How can we expect, even with "dynamic leadership," the basic structures of local government to reform themselves?

By contrast, Dahl is not even sure that dynamic leadership *is* lacking in the American community, and points to such men as Lee of New Haven, Dilworth of Philadelphia, and Daley of Chicago. He agrees that there is inequality of power in American society, but denies that the political sector has lost power to other sectors, particularly to business. In fact, it is Dahl's contention that the power-structure of American society has been moving steadily away from the monolithic type, which it more nearly resembled in the early part of the nineteenth century than it does in mid-twentieth century. What Dahl finds is a pluralism marked by fragmented, minority participation. In part, this seems to be a concomitant of increased bureaucratization. There are myriad decisions to be made, and no individual or power elite could possibly have the time, much less the knowledge, to control these many and major decisions. In this regard, Dahl notes the example of businessmen who may be instrumental in raising the money for United Fund and such organizations, but who have little if any say in how the money will be spent. The later decisions are made by social welfare agents, whose authority must be presumed to be legitimate in this area, if for no other reason than that so many Americans are willing to contribute one of their most valued possessions, money, to these agencies. Dahl wonders if raising the money is as important as deciding how it will be spent. Perhaps the crucial issue is whether or not the allocation of funds is of relevance to the businessmen. If in fact they have no interest in, or are satisfied with, the allocations, their lack of concern may reflect not their weakness or fear of defeat, but the realization that there is little power challenge involved.

That knowledge is power is implied in another argument by Dahl in challenge of Miller's thesis. Dahl contends that the use of influence has its cost. To exert one's influence and to lose may mean both loss of self-confidence and, more importantly, a loss of public prestige. Individuals are not prone to gamble away their prestige in areas where their competence may be questioned. And not only may their competence, but through this the legitimacy of their actions, be called into question. Here Dahl and Drucker would seem to be opposing Miller in their view of power in American society. Miller contends that complex and important decisions must be made every day in American communities, but the political leaders are uncertain, insecure; they don't know how far the limits of governmental authority extend. They don't have a clear conception of themselves as powerful men who can do things, who have the authority to initiate programs. Rather, they wait for others to act, to give them the cue, to tell them what to do and what not to do. And the people themselves don't know what they want of their government. They have been brought up to fear big government, and they have only a vague awareness of the extent and importance of the issues facing them. In this situation, the businessmen step in and act. This, after all, should not be surprising. Businessmen have a clearly defined self-image: They know that they have been chiefly responsible for the remarkable growth and prosperity of this country. They know that their values permeate all facets of American life. They know that what is good for business is good for the community. They are not trying to coerce anyone, or to be unduly influential. They are merely offering their advice where it is most needed.

Dahl says flatly that this is not what happens, that professionals and government officials often take action which is opposed by the businessmen, and that the former are the victors, with businessmen the losers. Drucker also insists that power is more widely diffused than Miller would have us believe.

One further aspect of the problem must be noted here. The political and other institutional sectors of social life have never in history been separate, disparate entities. In fact, in nonliterate societies they often formed one more or less homogeneous unit, so that it was almost impossible to separate one aspect from the other. The significant change in our time is that we are witnessing a conscious struggle by men representing various institutional sectors for control of the political power-center. At the same time men in the political center are striving to increase their control over those areas of life covered by the other centers. The struggle is carried on always in the name of democracy. Those who believe in limited government as the only guarantee of democracy attempt to limit the power of government, to limit the areas of life over which the government has control. Those who believe that the uncontrolled power of business, A.M.A., and the labor unions among other is the real danger to democracy, attempt to increase the power of government, to increase government's control over these other centers. Drucker is worried because there is so much power now vested in all of these organizations that he wonders if power can be kept under control at all. Miller worries because he sees business winning out in the struggle to dominate government, and Dahl worries because the public has been so generally uninterested in the struggle which involves its very existence.

There is no more complex and irksome problem facing this democracy than how power shall be distributed and controlled. We are harried because the decisions to be made are myriad and the amount of knowledge needed to be able to reduce alternatives to a single course of action would have been unthinkable in any previous era. We are further harried because those in authority, who have the right to make the decisions, to reduce alternatives, may not have the knowledge required to do so. Those with knowledge may be beyond popular control, and even beyond the control of those in authority. They may be able to exert great influence without accountability. How to bring influence and authority back under the same roof where they can both be controlled becomes our problem. The difficulty is compounded by the fact that there is in American society a tendency to deny that power exists, or to refuse to recognize the nature and ubiquity of power in human interaction. Life cannot proceed unless decisions are made and action programs carried out. But decision-making always implies that there is a plurality of courses of action open to the participants, and they must choose one from among these. The process of choice necessarily involves the use of influence, if not of coercion, even in the political decisions made by elected executives. Clearly, we must learn new techniques to control the distribution and exercise of political power in a community "which abhors its existence, disavows its possession, but values its exercise."[6]

FREEDOM

It has become clear in our time that freedom cannot mean a complete lack of restraint on behavior: To be a participant in human society is to have your behavior restrained in one form or another.[7] From the very moment of birth the child is fettered; his basic needs cannot be satisfied by himself alone. Left to his own resources he will not develop into a human being at all in the normal sense of that term as studies of feral and motherless children clearly show. Indeed, motherless children have a great deal of difficulty just trying to survive physically.[8] The

[6] For an incisive discussion of the American image of power see John K. Galbraith, *American Capitalism: The Concept of Countervailing Power* (Boston: Houghton Mifflin, 1952).

[7] Cogent discussions of liberty and freedom may be found in: John S. Mill, *On Liberty* (New York: Liberal Arts Press, 1956); Thomas I. Cook, "Individual Liberty Today: Challenge and Prospect," in Morrow Berger, *et al.* (eds)., *Freedom and Control in Modern Society* (Princeton: Van Nostrand, 1954); E. Abramson, H. A. Cutter, R. W. Kautz, and M. Mendelson, "Social Power and Commitment, A Theoretical Statement," *American Sociological Review,* XXIII (1958), 15-22.

[8] See for example, Kingsley Davis, "Final Note on a Case of Extreme Isolation," *American Journal of Sociology,* LII (1947), 432-37, and R. A. Spitz, "Hospitalism: An Inquiry into the Genesis of Psychiatric Conditions in Early Childhood," in *The Psychoanalytic Study of the Child* (New York: International Universities Press), I (1945), 53-74, and II (1946), 113-17.

very process of socialization by which the child grows to become an accepted member of the group and community is one of learning to conform to the beliefs, values, and sentiments of those concerned with the life of the individual. All of us are in large measure conforming individuals playing roles of father, mother, husband, wife, teacher, student, lawyer, businessman. We spend our day doing and saying what people expect us to do and to say. We are restrained consciously and unconsciously on every side. Even Thoreau was not free from these constraints in seeking his solitary way at Walden Pond. Perhaps his freedom was limited finally not so much by the fact that he couldn't escape entirely the money economy of the larger society, but by the fact that in order to communicate his experiences and to express his ideas, he had to use the language which society had furnished him. The very symbols of language limited what he saw and the way in which he interpreted what he saw. Nevertheless, Thoreau comes down to us as an individual, a person who achieved a greater degree of freedom from the fetters of society than most men of his time or of any other time in human history. And he reminds us that the struggle between the individual's freedom and group conformity is not peculiar to our time in history.[9] But if the social facts of life restrict us on every side, wherein lies freedom? It certainly does not lie in freeing oneself from power, from authority, influence and coercion, although this seems to have been a major aim of Americans during the past three centuries. Freedom must in fact lie in the ability of the individual to make choices, to be able to choose between alternative lines of action.

Seen in this light, freedom is very closely related to democracy and power. For the ability to make choices presumes that man is a responsible human being; as the political scientist Thomas Cook states, social conditioning does not remove all

[9] Henry David Thoreau, *Walden* and "Civil Disobedience," Mentor edition (New York: New American Library, 1959).

responsibility from the individual.[10] As pointed out above, democracy provides better guarantees than any other political system that the individual will have alternatives between which to choose. This assumption that man is morally responsible, and that he can make choices is at the heart of the Judaeo-Christian tradition, but only gradually have we come to perceive the social process which frames those choices.

There are two further aspects of the problem of freedom which merit attention here. They are: the extent or scope of social life within which it is relevant to talk about freedom; and the nature of restraint and how this affects freedom. A major concern of the history of post-feudal man has been his struggle to free himself from the control of church and state. The impetus to private interpretation of the Scriptures which arose out of the Protestant Reformation was at least a strong supporting factor to the notions of laissez-faire economics which developed gradually in the United States. If individual freedom lay in private interpretation of a direct and highly personal relationship with God, and if economic freedom lay in the pursuit of one's private interests in the marketplace, it was not illogical to expect that government would be looked upon with suspicion and scorn. The idea that "that government governs best which governs least" was a logical corollary of the former ideas. Thus freedom came to rest in freedom from the formal authority of church and state. The Reformation led to the first, as witness the fact that in 1950 there were 250 Protestant denominations in the United States. To insure freedom in the second, the checks and balances theory of government was put to the practical test, and government was to be the direct instrument of the people. For the rest people were free. But were they? Could people be free when they lived at subsistence levels? When they worked 70 hours a week under conditions which a boss and not they themselves could specify? The gradual breakdown of

[10]   Thomas Cook, *op. cit.*

the theory of laissez-faire economics and the growth of the theory that freedom, if it is to exist at all, must be somehow related to economics as well as politics and religion leads us to our present dilemma. However, we must first consider the nature of the restraints which the group imposes on us, and how these affect our approach to freedom.

It seems that prior to this century men sought mainly to free themselves from external constraints, from the constraints imposed by formal laws and group norms. It was generally assumed that internal constraints were a matter of the individual's innate conscience, and that once external constraints were eliminated, then the conscience would be free to make the right choices. We realize today that both internal and external constraints arise out of man's social situation, and that his freedom is inevitably conditioned by the degree of consistency between these two types of constrains.

But man is no mere automaton; he does not always and passively make the choice prescribed by the group code. Indeed, if he had always done this, there would have been little or no change in human behavior; literally, there would have been no history. The freedom to make choices has revealed that man can create new choices out of the presently existing ones, to provide for himself an ever increasing array of alternatives. At the same time he is also creating new patterns of conformity, new and varied restrictions on his behavior. There would seem to be a constant struggle between the tendency to increase freedom on the one hand and to increase power and control over the individual on the other hand. It is to various aspects of this struggle that Drucker, Dahl, and Miller have addressed themselves.

Drucker is deeply concerned that the growth of so many semiautonomous power-centers threatens to engulf the individual. How can the individual maintain his freedom in the face of these power-centers? Can they be made to serve him? At the same time, he recognizes that the individual sixty years ago was not very free either. He was restrained then by custom and tradition, a harsh nature, and poverty. But the question remains as to whether he is more or less free today.

The organization man is constrained externally in a variety of ways, which Drucker refers to as the "golden fetters." The organization means well, it protects him from cradle to grave. It offers stock bonuses, insurance policies, pension plans, and country club membership. While these offer man freedom from want and insecurity, and so guarantee him more alternatives in the economic realm, they may also have less desirable consequences. The individual may accept these much as the peasant accepted the *noblesse oblige* of the feudal lord. He may be giving away his power to govern himself not only in these areas but in others of greater importance. The labor union or the corporation or the university may demand loyalty and allegiance in return for economic security. But the individual owes to his job only the honest and most competent performance of a task, not undying loyalty. For to give the latter is to give away the ultimate safeguard to freedom.

Drucker recognizes that bureaucratic organization has brought many benefits to man and offers him many more, if he will not lose faith in his ability to control these new giants. He also reminds the individual that he can create an area of personal freedom that is inalienably his — "an independent sphere of accomplishment, something in which he is not an 'employee' but his own boss, something in which he, rather than the organization, sets the goals and the standards."

Although Miller does not speak directly to the problem of individual freedom, it is possible to derive some interesting implications about freedom from his analysis of community power-structure. Miller would hold with Tocqueville that the stability of the democratic system is enhanced by broad-scale participation in local community affairs, particularly through local government. But in his own research Miller finds this participation to be more true of England than of the United

States. Miller, through his contention that business values dominate community life and that businessmen have an overbearing influence on community life, is led to the conclusion that the individual citizen is perforce committed to the values and beliefs of that segment of community life, the business segment. To the extent that he is so committed he then has either no alternatives, or at best limited alternatives, between which to choose, and thus no effective freedom. To protect the freedom we have, Miller argues, other segments of the community must oppose business, not because business is necessarily bad, but because effective opposition is a keynote of democracy and freedom. We need more alternatives and a greater variety of alternatives than business offers.

One final aspect of Miller's discussion deserves mention here. Miller offers suggestive but not conclusive evidence that the community has lost its former sense of internal social solidarity as a result of rapid growth in size and segmentation of function. He suggests that this has led to a sense of alienation in the individual. To the extent that the individual used to depend on his community for a sense of identity, he may be less secure today. Of course, it may be that this sense of community identity has been replaced by a sense of organizational identity. However, the individual who cannot identify himself clearly with any significant group may lack the essential basis upon which his freedom will be built. The sociologist Nelson Foote, in another context, has suggested, "when doubt of identity creeps in, action is paralyzed."[11]

Dahl's analysis would lead us to conclude that the citizen has greater political freedom today than ever before in American society, since while power is still unequally distributed, the inequality is no longer cumulative. Those who have wealth are not necessarily the ones who control the vote, or the dom-

[11] Nelson Foote, "Identification as the Basis for a Theory of Motivation," *American Sociological Review,* XVI (1951), 14-22.

inant political party, or important administrative committees among other political resources. More people, absolutely and proportionately, are participating in decision-making in American society than ever before, and this means that more people have effective political freedom than ever before. There may not be a wide variety of choices, and often the alternatives between which the people may choose have been preselected by a small minority, yet still they do have choices which were never available to them in earlier periods. Whether or not the people make use of the freedom offered to them, the fact is that the system has gradually evolved into one in which these freedoms are possible.

Large numbers of Americans have exercised their freedom by not participating in political life. Dahl and others have argued that this is not without its advantages for the stability of a democratic society. Among other things it means that seldom will there be a cleavage of such proportions that the very stability of the system will be called into question. But there are other important implications. To exercise one's freedom effectively an individual must have some knowledge about the issue before him and the nature of the alternatives and their possible consequences. True freedom presupposes knowledge — but most of the citizens have little knowledge about the many issues which arise within their society and between their society and others. To what extent are they then free — given such limits on their knowledge?

The fact that a significant proportion of Americans stay away from the polls on election day may in fact mean that these people have most effectively exercised their freedom through nonparticipation. The consequence of such nonparticipation is that people may wake up some day to find that they have handed over their freedom to a small oligarchy. While nonparticipation may be a free and open alternative for the individual, it is equally the case that the individual is *not* free to give up his right to such participation. Political freedom in a democracy does not entail the right to give it up. If this were the case then democracy would in no small measure be self-defeating. Here however, Dahl and Drucker, certainly, and perhaps even Miller, would argue that the evidence of history points to a trend in the other direction, that is, of more and more participation by ever larger numbers of citizens. But this is no automatic and certain process, and by no means irreversible.

Democracy in America has developed gradually, employing a set of ground rules that insist on a basic consensus within a context of conflict. There has always been, and most assuredly always will be, alternative ways to resolve the many problems which beset society. The challenge which the democratic system poses for man is that it recognizes the inevitability of conflict over ways to solve problems, and at the same time provides man with a set of ground rules by which he can maximize the conflict without having major resort to coercion, and by which power can be controlled and diffused, but not eliminated.

The democratic system moreover places the greatest demands on the use of reason and the development of adequate knowledge by which means alone the largest number may not only remain free but increase their own personal freedom. At the same time the large-scale bureaucratic organization, in the form of the corporation, the trade union, the state university, and the hospital, among others, has arisen to challenge the viability of this democratic system. There is no question about whether a large bureaucratic organization can function effectively under a totalitarian or oligarchic political system; the question is whether it can function effectively under a democratic system. Or to put the matter the other way around, can a democratic system function under conditions of large-scale bureaucracy? To the extent that the bureaucratic organization is supposed to foster the spirit of achievement on the basis of technical competence, to the extent to which it thrives on knowledge, clarifies and delimits the sphere of authority and creates a specific role for the individual beyond which he is not bound to the organization, the answer must be in the affirmative. All of these elements of bureaucracy can strengthen the democratic system. We cannot take it for granted, however, that it will necessarily happen. The coming of the large-scale bureaucracy has brought many changes in the power-arrangements of our society, and we must understand these new power-arrangements to be able fully to comprehend the tasks which face our democracy in the years ahead. Therefore, we turn now to a brief discussion of key aspects of these power-arrangements.

POWER-ARRANGEMENTS IN AMERICAN SOCIETY

With the breakdown of the feudal order, there emerged the belief that the religious, political, and economic aspects of life were somehow distinct and autonomous spheres. The concomitant growth of an "egalitarian ethic," moreover, led to the conception of power over people, of any sort, as evil. At the same time there was also engendered the further belief that power over things was the proper pursuit for man. The exponents of rugged individualism failed to realize that power over things meant power over people, and that they were in fact exerting the same kind of unrestrained power which they rejected in religious and political authorities. As a result, effective control over the lives of the American people came to be centered in the economic system. The political system was simply kept weak and subordinated to the interests of economics.[12] But the means for political power were never destroyed, and in fact the potential for power in the government was gradually strengthened. It was the breakdown of the economic system in the period of the 1930's that finally brought into the open the challenge to the beliefs of the laissez-faire economists. With the New Deal and Franklin Roosevelt came the emergence of government as a contestant

[12]   Alpheus Thomas Mason, "Business Organized as Power," in Henry A. Turner (ed.), *Politics in the United States* (New York: McGraw-Hill, 1955).

with business for power over the lives of people in community and society.

The people have more and more turned to government as the sector which was most responsive to their needs, and gradually became aware of the potential of political power that was within their control. The response of American business has been to attempt to counter the power of government by providing a "welfare capitalism" for the people. Thus, they set about showing how business could protect the American from the cradle to the grave. It was assumed that business concern was automatically superior to governmental concern because those in the employ of government must of necessity be incompetent and constrained by bureaucratic red tape. Yet, given the nature of the problem involved, the same kind of bureaucratic system must be set up, whether within government or within business. Furthermore, the fact remains that if the people choose, they can have some control over their government; the government at all levels is still responsible to the people to some extent. The same is not true of corporate business in the United States.

The struggle for power over community and society is a continual one; but it is a struggle which seems now in the United States to be largely confined to the business and government sectors. On the horizon may be seen the professional educators, the new class of white-collar administrators, and perhaps labor, but they are not yet in the thick of battle. Nor is it clear that they will emerge as an independent sector or sectors.

Moreover, as long as people remain highly suspicious of government at any level, they may look to the business system for leadership. It is a fact of common experience that we question the tax on a package of cigarettes, not the business cost; we are apt to complain against the tax on a gallon of gasoline, not on the business part of the total price; we question the tax on our house and property, not the interest rate which we pay on our mortgage. Yet as citizens we have more control over the tax dollar than we do over the business dollar. And, as Dahl has suggested, we probably get more for our tax dollar than we do for our business dollar.[13] We should not be surprised, however, if the businessmen dominate the local community. Success in our society is largely defined in their terms. To whom else should the community look?

The contention that power is concentrated in the business sector of the community has been strongly disputed by Dahl in the preceding chapters of this book, and by others elsewhere.[14] The evidence from their studies suggests no definite structure of business domination but rather a diffused pattern of power. Put simply, the variety, scope, and complexity of issues mitigate against domination of the community by a single sector within it. Not only that, but the business interests themselves are by no means united on every issue. Surely, at the very least, both Dahl and Miller would agree that the business sectors of most communities have the greatest potential for control over the community decision-making process.

The foregoing analysis has revealed a process of tension and change in the power-arrangements of American society. On the one hand, there has been a diffusion of power resulting from the conscious and concerted effort of those who fear the power of government. This diffusion of power has also been in part a result of the growth of large-scale bureaucratic organization. On the other hand, power has increasingly become concentrated within limited sectors of society, particularly business. But the increasing concentration of power has neither been one-sided nor gone uncontested. In fact, the increasing sphere of power of the

[13] See also, John K. Galbraith, *The Affluent Society* (New York: Houghton, Mifflin, 1958).

[14] Daniel Bell, "The Power Elite—Reconsidered," *American Journal of Sociology*, LXIV (1958), 238-50; Nelson W. Polsby, "The Sociology of Community Power: A Reassessment," *Social Forces*, XXXVII (1959), 232-36; Polsby, "Three Problems in the Analysis of Community Power," *American Sociological Review*, XXIV (1959), 796-803; Raymond E. Wolfinger, "Reputation and Reality in the Study of Community Power," *American Sociological Review*, XXV (1960), 636-44.

federal government in recent years gives testimony to this conflict. It is also apparent that while this contest between concentration and diffusion of power forms a central focus of contemporary American politics, it has not yet come down to the state and local levels.

At the same time that this contest proceeds, we can note the tendency of some sectors of society to withdraw from the political decision-making process. The consequences of this abdication of power for political democracy have yet to be assessed. Certainly any adequate assessment must take into account the related problem of alienation.

ALIENATION AND DEMOCRACY

The independent development of a concern with the political and social consequences of alienation by all of our contributors reflects the importance and centrality of this concept to those engaged in political-sociological analysis. Clearly, alienation is a sponge concept absorbing a variety of empirical phenomena under its heading.[15] Yet there is some consensus on the forms of alienation which need to be invoked in this kind of analysis —normlessness, powerlessness, and self-estrangement.

Normlessness has been used, especially by Miller, in a dual manner to refer to the lack of clarity of the norms of community and political behavior, and to the belief that the normative means for achieving social goals are inadequate. Powerlessness, a theme running throughout this book, has reference to the individual's perception that the outcome of political events is beyond his control. Finally, self-estrangement refers to the discrepancy between personal ideals and social commitments: to the degree that an individual's ideals—from matters of self-conception through ideological preferences—are dissonant with the lines of action one is committed to through membership in specific social

[15] See Melvin Seeman, "On the Meaning of Alienation," *American Sociological Review,* XXIV (1959), 783-91.

groups, we may say that that person is self-estranged.

Why is it, we must ask, that these kinds of psychological variables are of concern to a constitutional lawyer, a sociologist, and a political scientist? Certainly this concern is not with these psychological dimensions as such, for this is not the level of analysis on which they have chosen to operate. Their concern, rather, is with the potential *social* consequences that these forms of alienation may lead to. Specifically, the hypothesis has been advanced that alienation, in any of its forms, leads to a vulnerability to antidemocratic appeals.[16] The alienated individual, isolated from the community, estranged from himself, and powerless to control his environment, may seek refuge in the order, clarity, and sense of mission provided by the authoritarian social movement. The sociologist Alvin Gouldner, in commenting on the functions of leadership in such movements, has said:

> When leadership is invoked today, often what is being asked for implicitly are men who can accomplish what the alienated individual, overcome by a sense of powerlessness, feels he cannot. The leader becomes the symbol of control and mastery, of knowledge and insight, denied the masses. One may remember a pre-Nazi song of German workers which went: "We are like marbles rolled against the wall." The anxiety-motored drive for security, evoked by a mass sense of powerlessness, finds outlets in a quest for dependence upon leadership.[17]

The quest for dependence is clearly antithetical to the quest for autonomy and freedom which must characterize the democratic society. The hazards for democracy of the conditions which produce alienation cannot be overlooked.

[16] This hypothesis constitutes one of the major themes of William Kornhauser's *The Politics of Mass Society* (Glencoe: Free Press, 1959).

[17] Alvin W. Gouldner (ed.) *Studies in Leadership* (New York: Harper and Bros., 1950), p. 7.

DEMOCRACY IN PERSPECTIVE

Knowledge is not only power, but it is the key to freedom and thus to the maintenance of democratic society. Freedom lies in our ability to make choices, to choose between alternatives. But how can we make choices when we have incomplete knowledge of alternatives or their consequences? Choice based on ignorance or half-truths is not freedom. The complex technology of peace and war made possible by the advances of modern science requires more, not less, knowledge of each individual in a democratic society. How is our technology to be used? We cannot leave to others these decisions. But we cannot possibly act effectively if we do not have a level of intellectual competence in social matters that matches our new levels of technological competence.

The highest degree of freedom which man can achieve in social matters is to be able to examine the alternatives available to him in an issue, and finding them unsatisfactory, create a new alternative for solution. Those with greater knowledge will have more influence and hence, more power than others. We must not fear this. We have too long labored under the false impression that democracy meant a completely equal sharing of knowledge, on the assumption that this constituted a guarantee of social equality. Surely, Dahl's measured analysis of the problem of equality has demonstrated the falseness of this view.

Formal education as we know it today certainly falls far short of the goal of preparing people to cope creatively with our complex civilization. Education per se is not, and can not be, the panacea that the early spokesmen for democracy envisioned. Yet, where else can we begin to look? Clearly what is needed is an educational revolution — a revolution of the scope and impact of the many technological revolutions that have led to the development of the large-scale urban-industrial societies of today. The signs that such a revolution has begun already exist.

In the final analysis, what makes democracy such a difficult political system to maintain and develop is the very nature of the demands which it makes upon those who wish to practice it. Because a democratic system attempts to achieve a maximum diffusion of power within a system of order, and thus tries to maximize personal freedom, it is at best slow-moving and halting in its attempts to come to grips with the problems which constantly confront it. Power, grounded in knowledge and framed by respect for human dignity, is the necessary tool for the development of the democratic system.

SELECTED BIBLIOGRAPHY
IN
POLITICAL SOCIOLOGY

1955 - 1960

Certainly a measure of our success with any individual reader will be the stimulation we have provided to explore further this area of political sociology. While political scientists, sociologists and philosophers have long been concerned with the analysis of power and the regulative institutions of society, concerted effort in the empirical study of these phenomena from a political-sociological perspective is a recent development. We offer here a selected bibliography of the most current concerns of political sociologists. Our bibliography is by no means exhaustive, and while we have emphasized empirical studies we have attempted to include the more important theoretical discussions of this time-period. Some earlier works which were cited in the preceding chapters have also been included.

Our selections have been made in response to the desire to provide the reader with the most salient writings dealing with the themes probed in this book. These include the nature of power, democracy, freedom, studies and critiques of community power, voting behavior, alienation, and problems of bureaucracy.

W.V.D.
H.J.E.

153

BOOKS

Adrian, Charles R. *Governing Urban America: Structure, Politics, and Administration*. New York: McGraw-Hill, 1955.

Albig, William. *Modern Public Opinion*. New York: McGraw-Hill, 1956.

Angell, Robert C. *Free Society and Moral Crisis*. Ann Arbor: University of Michigan Press, 1958.

Apter, David E. *The Gold Coast in Transition*. Princeton: Princeton University Press, 1955.

Bain, Henry M., Jr., and Hecock, Donald S. *Ballot Position and Voters Choice*. Detroit: Wayne State University Press, 1957.

Banfield, Edward C. *Political Influence*. Glencoe, Ill.: The Free Press, 1960.

Barber, Bernard. *Social Stratification: A Comparative Analysis of Structure and Process*. New York: Harcourt, Brace, 1957.

Becker, Howard and Boskoff, Alvin (eds.). *Modern Sociological Theory in Continuity and Change*. New York: The Dryden Press, 1957.

Bell, Daniel (ed). *The New American Right*. New York: Criterion Books, 1955.

Bell, Daniel. *The End of Ideology*. Glencoe: The Free Press, 1960.

Bendix, Reinhard. *Max Weber: An Intellectual Portrait*. Garden City, N.Y.: Doubleday, 1960.

_____. *Work and Authority in Industry*. New York: John Wiley and Sons, 1956.

Benney, M., Gray, A. P., and Rear, R. H. *How People Vote*. London: Routledge and Kegan Paul, 1956.

Berger, Morrow, Abel, Theodore, and Page, Charles H. *Freedom and Control in Modern Society; In Honor of Robert Morrison MacIver*. New York: Van Nostrand, 1954.

Berle, Adolf A., Jr. *Economic Power and Free Society*. New York: Fund for The Republic, 1957.

Binkley, Wilfred E. *American Political Parties, Their Natural History*. 3rd ed., rev. and enl. New York: Knopf, 1958.

Binkley, Wilfred E. and Moos, Malcolm C. *A Grammar of American Politics: The National, State and Local Governments*. 3rd ed., rev. New York: Knopf, 1958.

Blau, Peter. *Bureaucracy in Modern Society*. New York: Random House, 1956.

Brookings Institution. *Research Frontiers in Politics and Government, Brookings Lectures, 1955*. Washington D.C.: Brookings Institution, 1955.

Bryson, Lyman, Faust, Clarence H., Finkelstein, Louis and Mac-
    Iver, R. M. (eds.). *Aspects of Human Equality*. New York:
    Harper and Bros., 1957.
Brzezinski, Zbigniew. *Totalitarian Dictatorship and Autocracy*.
    Cambridge, Mass.: Harvard University Press, 1956.
Burdick, Eugene and Brodbeck, Arthur J. (eds.). *American Voting
    Behavior*. Glencoe, Ill.: The Free Press, 1959.
Burlingame, Roger. *The American Conscience*. New York: Knopf,
    1957.
Burns, James MacGregor, and Peltason, Jack Walter. *Government
    By the People: The Dymanics of American National, State,
    and Local Government*. 3rd ed. Englewood Cliffs, N. J.: Pren-
    tice-Hall, 1957.
Campbell, Angus, Converse, Philip E., Miller, Warren E., and
    Stokes, Donald E. *The American Voter*. New York: John Wiley
    and Sons, 1960.
Campbell, Angus and Cooper, Homer C. *Group Differences in
    Attitudes and Votes*. Ann Arbor: Survey Research Center,
    The University of Michigan, 1956.
Chaffee, Zechariah. *The Blessings of Liberty*. Philadelphia: Lip-
    pincott, 1956.
Coleman, James S. *Community Conflict*. Glencoe, Ill.: The Free
    Press, 1957.
Cornell University. *Cornell Studies in Civil Liberties*. Ithaca, N. Y.:
    Cornell University Press, 1946-1957.
Coser, Lewis A. *The Functions of Social Conflict*. Glencoe, Ill.:
    The Free Press, 1956.
Cottrell, William F. *Energy and Society; The Relation Between
    Energy, Social Change, and Economic Dev.......* New
    York: McGraw-Hill, 1955.
Curti, Merle. *American Paradox*. New Brunswick, N. J.: Rutgers
    University Press, 1956.
Curti, Merle, assisted by Daniel, Robert, Livermore, Shaw, Jr., Van-
    Hise, Joseph and Curti, Margaret M. *The Making of an
    American Community*. Stanford, Calif.: Stanford University
    Press, 1959.
Cushman, Robert E. *Civil Liberties in the United States: A Guide
    to Current Problems and Experience*. Ithaca, N.Y.: Cornell
    University Press, 1956.
Dahl, Robert A. *A Preface To Democratic Theory*. Chicago: Uni-
    versity of Chicago Press, 1956.
Dahrendorf, Ralf. *Class and Class Conflict*. Stanford, Calif.: Stan-
    ford University Press, 1959.

Davidson, Donald, Suppes, Patrick, and Siegel, Sidney. *Decision-Making: An Experimental Approach.* Stanford, Calif.: Stanford University Press, 1957.

Dobriner, William M. (ed.). *The Suburban Community.* New York: G. P. Putnam's Sons, 1958.

Douglas, Elisha P. *Rebels and Democrats.* Chapel Hill: University of North Carolina Press, 1955.

Downs, Anthony. *An Economic Theory of Democracy.* New York: Harper and Bros., 1957.

Drucker, Peter F. *America's Next Twenty Years.* New York: Harper and Bros., 1957.

————. *Landmarks of Tomorrow.* New York: Harper and Bros., 1959.

Durkheim, Emile. *Professional Ethics and Civic Morals.* Trans. and edited by Cornelia Brookfield. Glencoe, Ill.: The Free Press, 1958.

Ekirch, Arthur A. *The Decline of American Liberalism.* New York: Longmans, Green, 1955.

Eulau, Heinz, Eldersveld, Samuel J., and Janowitz, Morris (eds.). *Political Behavior.* Glencoe, Ill.: The Free Press, 1956.

Fagley, Richard M. *The Population Explosion and Christian Responsibility.* New York: Oxford University Press, 1960.

Fisher, Robert M. (ed.). *The Metropolis in Modern Life.* New York: Doubleday, 1955.

Form, William H. and Miller, Delbert C. *Industry, Labor and Community.* New York: Harper and Bros., 1960.

The Editors of *Fortune.* *The Exploding Metropolis.* Garden City, N.Y.: Doubleday, 1958.

Frankel, Charles. *The Case for Modern Man.* New York: Harper and Bros., 1955.

Freidrich, Carl J. *Authority.* Cambridge, Mass.: Harvard University Press, 1958.

Friedmann, W. *Law in a Changing Society.* Berkeley, Calif.: University of California Press, 1959.

Fuchs, Lawrence H. *The Political Behavior of American Jews.* Glencoe, Ill.: The Free Press, 1956.

Galbraith, John K. *The Affluent Society.* New York: Houghton, Mifflin, 1958.

Ginsberg, Morris. *Essays in Sociology and Social Philosophy.* Vol. I, *On The Diversity of Morals.* New York: Macmillan, 1957.

Gittler, Joseph B. (ed.). *Review of Sociology: Analysis of a Decade.* New York: John Wiley and Sons, 1957.

Gordon, Milton M. *Social Class in American Sociology.* Durham,

N.C.: Duke University Press, 1958.

Gouldner, Alvin (ed.). *Studies in Leadership*. New York: Harper and Bros., 1950.

Graham, George A. *America's Capacity to Govern*. Tuscaloosa: University of Alabama Press, 1960.

Greer, Scott. *Last Man In: Racial Access to Union Power*. Glencoe, Ill.: The Free Press, 1959.

Grimes, Alan P. *American Political Thought*. New York: Holt, 1955.

Gross, Feliks. *The Seizure of Political Power in a Century of Revolution*. New York: Philosophical Library, 1958.

Guetzkow, Harold. *Multiple Loyalties: Theoretical Approach to a Problem in International Organization*. Princeton: Princeton University Press, 1955.

Harding, Arthur L. (ed.). *Responsibility in Law and in Morals*. Dallas: Southern Methodist University Press, 1960.

Hartz, Louis. *The Liberal Tradition in America: An Interpretation of American Political Thought Since the Revolution*. New York: Harcourt, Brace, 1955.

Hauser, Philip M. (ed.). *Population and World Politics*. Glencoe, Ill.: The Free Press, 1958.

Hawley, Amos H. *The Changing Shape of Metropolitan America*. Glencoe, Ill.: The Free Press, 1956.

Heady, Ferrell, and Stokes, Sybil L. *Comparative Public Administration: A Selected Annotated Bibliography*. 2nd ed. Ann Arbor: Institute of Public Administration, The University of Michigan, 1960.

Hobsbawm, E. J. *Social Bandits and Primitive Rebels*. Glencoe, Ill.: The Free Press, 1959.

Hunter, Floyd. *Top Leadership, U.S.A.* Chapel Hill: University of North Carolina Press, 1959.

Hunter, Floyd, Schaffer, Ruth C. and Sheps, Cecil G. *Community Organization: Action and Inaction*. Chapel Hill: University of North Carolina Press, 1956.

Hyman, Herbert H. *Political Socialization*. Glencoe, Ill.: The Free Press, 1959.

International Sociological Association, in collaboration with Bernard, Jessie, Pear, T. H., Aron, Raymond, and Angell, Robert C. *The Nature of Conflict: Studies on the Sociological Aspects of International Tensions*. Paris, France: UNESCO, 1957.

Janowitz, Morris (ed.). *Community Political Systems*. Glencoe, Ill.: The Free Press, 1960.

Janowitz, Morris. *The Professional Soldier*. Glencoe, Ill.: The Free

Press, 1960.

Janowitz, Morris and Marvick, Dwaine. *Competitive Pressure and Democratic Consent*. Ann Arbor: University of Michigan, 1956 (Michigan Governmental Studies No. 32, Bureau of Government, Institute of Public Administration).

Jennings, Eugene. *The Anatomy of Leadership: Princes, Heroes and Supermen*. New York: Harper and Bros., 1960.

Kahl, Joseph A. *The American Class Structure*. New York: Rinehart, 1957.

Katz, Elihu and Lazarsfeld, Paul F. *Personal Influence*. Glencoe, Ill.: The Free Press, 1955.

Kelley, Stanley, Jr. *Professional Public Relations and Political Power*. Baltimore: Johns Hopkins Press, 1956.

Kelly, Alfred H. (ed.). *Foundations of Freedom in the American Constitution*. New York: Harper and Bros., 1958.

Key, V.O. *Politics, Parties and Pressure Groups*. 4th ed. New York: Thomas Y. Crowell Co., 1958.

Konvitz, Milton R. *Fundamental Liberties of A Free People: Religion, Speech, Press, Assembly*. Ithaca: Cornell University Press, 1957.

Kornhauser, Arthur (ed.). *Problems of Power in American Democracy*. Detroit: Wayne State University Press, 1957.

Kornhauser, William. *The Politics of Mass Society*. Glencoe, Ill.: The Free Press, 1959.

Lane, Robert E. *Political Life*. Glencoe, Ill.: The Free Press, 1959.

Lee, Dorothy. *Freedom and Culture*. Englewood Cliffs, N.J.: Prentice-Hall, 1959.

Lerner, Daniel. *The Passing of Traditional Society*. Glencoe, Ill.: The Free Press, 1958.

Lerner, Max. *America as a Civilization*. New York: Simon and Schuster, 1957.

Lipset, S. M., Trow, M. and Coleman, J.S. *Union Democracy*. Glencoe, Ill.: The Free Press, 1956.

Loewenstein, Karl. *Political Power and the Governmental Process*. Chicago: University of Chicago Press, 1957.

Loomis, Charles P. *Social Systems: Essays on Their Persistence and Change*. Princeton: D. Van Nostrand Co., 1960.

Lubell, Samuel. *The Revolt of the Moderates*. New York: Harper and Bros., 1956.

Maass, Arthur (ed.). *Area and Power*. Glencoe, Ill.: The Free Press, 1959.

March, James G. and Simon, Herbert A. with the collaboration of Harold Guetzkow. *Organizations*. New York: John Wiley and

Sons, 1958.

Marvick, Elizabeth W. and Reiss, Albert J. *Community Life and Social Policy: Selected Papers by Louis Wirth*. Chicago: University of Chicago Press, 1956.

Mason, Alpheus Thomas (ed.). *Free Government in the Making: Readings in American Political Thought*. 2nd ed. New York: Oxford University Press, 1956.

Mayer, A.J. *When Labor Votes*. New York: University Books, 1956.

Meisel, James H. *The Myth of the Ruling Class: Gaetano Mosca and the Elite*. Ann Arbor: University of Michigan Press, 1958.

Melman, Seymour. *Decision Making and Productivity*. New York: John Wiley and Sons, 1958.

Merton, Robert K. *Social Theory and Social Structure*. Glencoe, Ill.: The Free Press, 1957.

Merton, Robert K., Broom, Leonard, and Cottrell, Leonard S., Jr. (eds.). *Sociology Today,* New York: Basic Books, 1959.

Meyer, Donald B. *The Protestant Search for Political Realism, 1919-1941*. Berkeley and Los Angeles: University of California Press, 1960.

Mighell, Ronald L. *American Agriculture: Its Structure and Place in the Economy*. New York: John Wiley and Sons, 1955.

Mills, C. Wright. *The Power Elite*. New York: Oxford University Press, 1956.

Moore, Barrington, Jr. *Political Power and Social Theory*. Cambridge: Harvard University Press, 1958.

Morgenthau, Hans J. *The Purpose of American Politics*. New York: Knopf, 1960.

Murray, John Courtney. *We Hold These Truths*. New York: Sheed and Ward, 1960.

MacIver, Robert. *The Web of Government*. New York: Macmillan, 1947.

MacRae, Duncan, Jr. *Dimensions of Congressional* Voting. Berkeley and Los Angeles: University of California Press, 1958.

McCloskey, Robert G. *The American Supreme Court*. Chicago: University of Chicago Press, 1960.

Nelson, Lowrey. *The Community: Its Structure and Changes*. New York: Macmillan, 1960.

Neumann, Franz. *The Democratic and the Authoritarian State*. Glencoe, Ill.: The Free Press, 1957.

Parsons, Talcott and Smelser, Neil J. *Economy and Society*. Glencoe, Ill.: The Free Press, 1956.

Pinner, Frank A., Jacobs, Paul, and Selznick, Philip. *Old Age and*

    Political Behavior: A Case Study. Berkeley: University of California Press, 1959.

Porter, Kirk H. and Johnson, Donald B., comps. *National Party Platforms, 1840-1956*. Urbana: University of Illinois Press, 1956.

Ranney, Austin and Kendall, Willmore. *Democracy and the American Party System*. New York: Harcourt, Brace, 1956.

Rose, Arnold M. (ed.). *The Institutions of Advanced Societies*. Minneapolis, Minn.: University of Minnesota Press, 1958.

Rossiter, Clinton L. *Conservatism in America*. New York: Knopf, 1955.

St. James, Warren D. *The National Association for the Advancement of Colored People, A Case Study in Pressure Groups*. New York: Exposition Press, 1958.

Schapera, L. *Government and Politics in Tribal Societies*. London: Watts, 1956.

Schattschneider, E. E. *The Semisovereign People: A Realist's View of Democracy in America*. New York: Holt, Rinehart, Winston, 1960.

Schermerhorn, Richard A. *Society and Power*. New York: Random House, 1961.

Schlesinger, Joseph A. *How They Became Governor*. East Lansing: Michigan State University Press, Government Research Bureau, Political Research Studies, No. 4, 1957.

Schramm, Wilbur. *Responsibility in Mass Communication*. New York: Harper and Bros., 1957.

Schubert, Glendon A. *Quantitative Analysis of Judicial Behavior*. Glencoe, Ill.: The Free Press, 1959.

Selekman, Sylvia and Selekman, Benjamin. *Power and Morality in a Business Society*. New York: McGraw-Hill, 1956.

Selznick, Philip. *Leadership in Administration*. Evanston: Row, Peterson and Co., 1957.

——————. *The Organizational Weapon*. Glencoe, Ill.: The Free Press, 1960.

Shannon, David A. *The Socialist Party of America: a History*. New York: Macmillan, 1955.

Shils, Edward A. *The Torment of Secrecy; The Background and Consequences of American Security Policies*. Glencoe, Ill.: The Free Press, 1956.

Simmel, Georg. *Conflict and the Web of Group-Affiliation*. Glencoe, Ill.: The Free Press, 1955.

Simon, Herbert A. *Models of Man: Social and Rational*. New York: John Wiley and Sons, 1957.

Smith, Howard R. *Democracy and the Public Interest.* Athens: University of Georgia Press, 1960.

Smith, James Morton. *Freedom's Fetters: The Alien And Sedition Laws and American Civil Liberties.* Ithaca: Cornell University Press, 1956.

Smith, M. Brewster, Bruner, Jerome S., and White, Robert W. *Opinions and Personality.* New York: John Wiley and Sons, 1956.

Smuckler, Ralph H. and Belknap, George M. *Leadersip and Participation in Urban Political Affairs.* East Lansing: Michigan State University, Government Research Bureau, Political Research Studies, No. 2, 1956.

Sower, Christopher, Holland, John, Tiedke, Kenneth, and Freeman, Walter. *Community Involvement.* Glencoe, Ill.: The Free Press, 1957.

Stein, M., Vidich, A. J., and White, D. M. (eds.). *Identity and Anxiety: Survival of the Person in Mass Society.* Glencoe, Ill.: The Free Press, 1960.

Stouffer, Samuel A. *Communism, Conformity, and Civil Liberties: A Cross-Section of the Nation Speaks Its Mind.* Garden City, N. Y.: Doubleday, 1955.

Strauss, Leo. *What Is Political Philosophy? and Other Studies.* Glencoe, Ill.: The Free Press, 1959.

Stroung-Hupe, Robert. *Power and Community.* New York: Praeger, 1956.

Sussman, Marvin (ed.). *Community Structure and Analysis.* New York: Thomas Y. Crowell Co., 1959.

Sutton, Francis X., Harris, S.E., and Kaysen, K. *The American Business Creed.* Cambridge: Harvard University Press, 1956.

Sweeney, Stephen B. (ed.), and Blair, George S. (assist. ed.). *Metropolitan Analysis.* Philadelphia: University of Pennsylvania Press, 1958.

Taylor, Telford. *Grand Inquest: The Story of Congressional Investigations.* New York: Simon and Schuster, 1955.

Turner, Henry A. (ed.). *Politics in the United States.* New York: McGraw-Hill, 1955.

Van Riper, Paul P. *History of the United States Civil Service.* Evanston, Ill.: Row, Peterson, 1958.

Verney, Douglas V. *The Analysis of Political Systems.* Glencoe, Ill.: The Free Press, 1960.

Vidich, Arthur J. and Bensman, Joseph. *Small Town in Mass Society: Class, Power and Religion in a Rural Community.* Princeton University Press, 1958.

Wahlke, John C. and Eulau, Heinz (eds.). *Legislative Behavior*. Glencoe, Ill.: The Free Press, 1959.

Warner, W. Lloyd and Abeglen, James C. *Big Business Leaders in America*. New York: Harper and Bros., 1955.

—————. *Occupational Mobility in American Business and Industry: 1928-1952*. Minneapolis, Minn.: University of Minnesota Press, 1955.

Wasserman, Paul and Silander, Fred S. *Decision-Making:An Annotated Bibliography*. Ithaca, N.Y.: Cornell University Graduate School of Business and Public Administration, 1958.

Weber, Max. *From Max Weber: Essays in Sociology*. Translated by H. Gerth and C. W. Mills. New York: Oxford University Press, 1946.

—————. *The Theory of Social and Economic Organization*. Translated by A. M. Henderson and Talcott Parsons. New York: Oxford University Press, 1947.

Weiss, Paul. *Our Public Life*. Bloomington, Ind.: Indiana University Press, 1959.

White, Leonard D. *Introduction to the Study of Public Administration*. 4th ed. New York: Macmillan, 1955.

White, Ralph K. and Lippitt, Ronald. *Autocracy and Democracy: An Experimental Inquiry*. New York: Harper and Bros., 1960.

Whyte, William H., Jr. *The Organization Man*. New York: Simon and Schuster, 1956.

Williams, Robin M., Jr. *American Society: A Sociological Interpretation*. New York: Knopf, 1960.

Wilson, James Q. *Negro Politics: The Search for Leadership*. Glencoe, Ill.: Free Press, 1960.

Wittfogel, Karl A. *Oriental Despotism: A Comparative Study of Total Power*. New Haven: Yale University Press, 1957.

Young, Roland. *The American Congress*. New York: Harper and Bros., 1958.

Young, Roland (ed.). *Approaches to the Study of Politics: Twenty-Two Contemporary Essays Exploring the Nature of Politics and Methods by Which It Can Be Studied*. Evanston, Ill.: Northwestern University Press, 1958.

Zetterberg, Hans L. (ed.). *Sociology in the United States of America: A Trend Report*. Paris, France: UNESCO, 1956.

ARTICLES

Adams, Stuart. "Origins of American Occupational Elites: 1900-1955," *American Journal of Sociology,* 62:360-68, 1957.

Adrian, Charles R., "A Typology for Nonpartisan Elections," *Western Political Quarterly,* 12:449-58, 1959.

——————. "Leadership and Decision-Making in Manager Cities: A Study of Three Communities," *Public Administration Review,* 18:208-13, 1958.

Agger, Robert. "Power Attributions in the Local Community: Theoretical and Research Considerations," *Social Forces,* 34:322-31, 1956.

Agger, R. and Goldrich, D. "Community Power Structures and Partisanship," *American Sociological Review,* 23:383-92, 1958.

Agger, R. and Ostrom, V. "The Political Structure of a Small Community," *Public Opinion Quarterly,* 20:81-89, 1956.

Almond, Gabriel A. "A Comparative Study of Interest Groups and the Political Process," *American Political Science Review,* 52:270-82, 1958.

Anderson, William. "Political Influences of the Metropolis," in R. M. Fisher (ed.), *The Metropolis in Modern Life.* New York: Doubleday, 1955.

Apter, David E. "A Comparative Method for the Study of Politics," *American Journal of Sociology,* 64:221-37, 1958.

Banfield, Edward C. "The Politics of Metropolitan Area Organization," *Midwest Journal of Political Science,* 1:77-91, 1957.

Barkley, R. "Theory of the Elite and the Mythology of Power," *Science and Society,* 19:97-106, 1955.

Barrett, Patricia. "Democracy in an Age of Technology," *Social Order,* 7:70-76, 1957.

Barth, E. "Power Structure and the Negro Sub-Community," *American Sociological Review,* 24:69-76, 1959.

Becker, Howard S. "Notes on the Concept of Commitment," *American Journal of Sociology,* 66:32-40, 1960.

Beer, Samuel H. "Group Representation in Britain and the United States," *Annals* of the American Academy of Political and Social Science, 319:130-40, 1958.

Belknap, George and Smuckler, R. "Political Power Relations in a Mid-West City," *Public Opinion Quarterly,* 20:73-81, 1956.

Bell, Daniel. "The Power-Elite Reconsidered," *American Journal of Sociology,* 64:238-50, 1958.

——————. "The Theory of the Mass Society," *Commentary,* 22:75-83, 1956.

Bendix, Reinhard. "A Study of Managerial Ideologies," *Economic Development and Cultural Change,* 5:118-28, 1957.

_____. "Industrialization, Ideologies, and Social Structure," *American Sociological Review,* 24:613-23, 1959.

Bendix, R. and Lipset, S. M. "Political Sociology — A Trend Report and Bibliography," *Current Sociology,* 6:79-169, 1957.

Bennett, E. B. "Discussion, Decision, Commitment, and Consensus in Group Decision," *Human Relations,* 3:251-73, 1955.

Berger, Morrow. "Bureaucracy East and West," *Administrative Science Quarterly,* 1:518-29, 1957.

_____. "The Business Elite: Then and Now," *Commentary,* 22:367-74, 1956.

Berle, Adolf A., Jr. "Concentration of Economic Power and Protection of Freedom of Expression," *Annals* of the American Academy of Political and Social Science, 300:20-28, 1955.

Bernard, Jessie. "Dimensions and Axes of Supreme Court Decisions: A Study in the Sociology of Conflict," *Social Forces,* 34:19-27, 1955.

Blackwell, Gordon. "Community Analysis" in R. Young (ed.), *Approaches to the Study of Politics.* Evanston, Ill., Northwestern University Press, 1958.

Brogan, D. W. "The End of Illusion?" *Yale Review,* 47:161-74, 1957.

Boskoff, Alvin. "General Sociological Theory and Political Phenomena: Structural-Functionalism at Work," *Alpha Kappa Deltan,* 29:70-73, 1959.

Braybrooke, D. "The Relevance of Norms to Political Description," *American Political Science Review,* 52:989-1006, 1958.

Bronfenbrenner, Martin. "Two Concepts of Economic Freedom," *Ethics,* 65: 157-70, 1955.

Brotz, Howard M. "Social Stratification and the Political Order," *American Journal of Sociology,* 64:571-78, 1959.

Brzezinski, Zbigniew. "Totalitarianism and Rationality," *American Political Science Review,* 50:757-63, 1956.

Buchanan, W. "An Inquiry into Purposive Voting," *Journal of Politics,* 18:281-96, 1956.

Bunzel, J. H. "The General Ideology of American Small Business," *Political Science Quarterly,* 70:87-102, 1955.

Campbell, Angus. "The Political Implication of Community Identification," in R. Young (ed.), *Approaches to the Study of Politics.* Evanston, Ill.: Northwestern University Press, 1958.

Campbell, Angus and Miller, Warren E. "The Motivational Basis of Straight and Split Ticket Voting," *American Political*

Science Review, 51:293-312, 1957.

Catlin, George E. G. "Political Theory: What Is It?" Political Science Quarterly, 72:1-29, 1957.

Chalmers, David M. "The Muckrakers and the Growth of Corporate Power: A Study in Constructive Journalism," American Journal of Economics and Sociology, 18:294-311, 1959.

Cohen, Julius, Robson, Reginald A. H., and Bates, Alan. "Ascertaining the Moral Sense of the Community," Journal of Legal Education, 8:137-49, 1955.

Cohen, Sanford. "Conservatism, Radicalism and Unionism," American Journal of Economics and Sociology, 16:127-43, 1957.

Cohn, Werner. "The Politics of the Jews," in Marshall Sklare (ed.), The Jews: Social Patterns of an American Group. Glencoe, Ill.: The Free Press, 1958.

Cole, A. B. "Social Stratification and Mobility: Some Political Implications," Annals of the American Academy of Political and Social Science, 308:121-29, 1956.

Coleman, John R. "The Compulsive Pressures of Democracy in Unionism," American Journal of Sociology, 61:519-28, 1956.

Cook, S. D. "Hacker's Liberal Democracy and Social Control: A Critique," American Political Science Review, 51:1027-39, 1957.

Coser, Lewis A. "Social Conflict and the Theory of Social Change," British Journal of Sociology, 8:197-207, 1957.

Cutright, Phillips and Rossi, Peter H. "Party Organization in Primary Elections," American Journal of Sociology, 64:262-69, 1958.

Dahl, Robert A. "A Critique of The Ruling Elite Model," American Political Science Review, 52: 463-69, 1958.

————. "Business and Politics: A Critical Appraisal of Political Science," American Political Science Review, 52:1-34, 1959.

————. "The Concept of Power," Behavioral Science, 2:201-214, 1957.

————. "Hierarchy, Democracy, and Bargaining in Politics and Economics," in Research Frontiers in Politics and Government, Brookings Lectures, 1955. Washington, D.C.: Brookings Institution, 1955.

Daiches, David. "Education in Democratic Society," Commentary, 23:336-43, 1957.

D'Antonio, W. V., Form, W. H., Loomis, C. P., and Erickson, E. C. "Institutional and Occupational Representations in Eleven Community Influence Systems," American Sociological Review, June 1961.

Davis, K. "The Political Impact of New Population Trends," *Foreign Affairs*, 36:293-301, 1958.

de Grazia, Alfred. "Nature and Prospects of Political Interest Groups," *Annals* of American Academy of Political and Social Science, 319:113-22, 1958.

Dexter, Lewis A. "Candidates Must Make the Issues and Give Them Meaning," *Public Opinion Quarterly*, 19:408-14, 1955-56.

_____. "What Do Congressmen Hear: The Mail," *Public Opinion Quarterly*, 20:16-17, 1956.

Dick, Harry R. "A Method for Ranking Community Influentials," *American Sociological Review*, 25:395-99, 1960.

Downs, Anthony. "An Economic Theory of Political Action in a Democracy," *Journal of Political Economy*, 65:135-50, 1957.

Drucker, Peter F. "Organized Religion and the American Creed," *Review of Politics*, 18:296-304, 1956.

Dubin, Robert. "Power and Union-Management Relations," *Administrative Science Quarterly*, 2:60-81, 1957.

DuBois, Cora. "The Dominant Value Profile of American Culture," *American Anthropologist*, 57:1232-39, 1955.

Durant, H. "Public Opinion, Polls and Foreign Policy," *British Journal of Sociology*, 6:149-58, 1955.

Easton, David. "An Approach to the Analysis of Political Systems," *World Politics*, 9:383-400, 1957.

_____. "Traditional and Behavioral Research in American Political Science," *Administrative Science Quarterly*, 2:110-15, 1957.

Eisenstadt, S. N. "Political Struggle in Bureaucratic Societies," *World Politics*, 9:15-36, 1956.

_____. "Sociological Aspects of Political Development in Underdeveloped Countries," *Economic Development and Cultural Change*, 5:289-307, 1957.

Elder, R. E. "The Public Studies Division of the Department of State: Public Opinion Analysis in the Formulation and Conduct of American Foreign Policy," *Western Political Quarterly*, 10:783-92, 1957.

Eldersveld, Samuel J. "Experimental Propaganda Techniques and Voting Behavior," *American Political Science Review*, 50:154-65, 1956.

_____. "Theory and Method in Voting Behavior Research," *Journal of Politics*, 13:70-87, 1951.

Epstein, L. D. "British Mass Parties in Comparison with American Parties," *Political Science Quarterly*, 71:97-125, 1956.

Eulau, Heinz H. "Identification with Class and Political Perspective," *Journal of Politics,* 18:232-53, 1956.

_____. "Identification with Class and Political Role Behavior," *Public Opinion Quarterly,* 20:515-29, 1956.

_____. "From Public Opinion to Public Philosophy: Walter Lippman's Classic Re-examined," *American Journal of Economics and Sociology,* 15:439-51, 1956.

Eulau, Heinz, Buchanan, W., Ferguson, L., Wahlke, J. C. "The Political Socialization of American State Legislators," *Midwest Journal of Political Science,* 3:188-206, 1959.

Fanelli, A. A. "A Typology of Community Leadership Based on Influence and Interaction within the Leader Sub-system," *Social Forces,* 34:332-38, 1956.

Farber, Maurice L. "The Anal Character and Political Aggression," *Journal of Abnormal Social Psychology,* 51:486-89. 1955.

Farris, C. D. " 'Authoritarianism' as a Political Behavior Variable," *Journal of Politics,* 18:61-82, 1956.

_____. "A Method of Determining Ideological Groupings in the Congress," *Journal of Politics,* 20:308-38, 1958.

Ferkiss, Victor C. "Populist Influence in American Fascism," *Western Political Quarterly,* 10:350-73, 1957.

Finer, S. E. "The Political Power of Private Capital, II," *Sociological Review,* 4:5-30, 1956.

Fitch, L. C. "Fiscal and Political Problems of Increasing Urbanization," *Political Science Quarterly,* 71:71-89, 1956.

Fitzgibbon, Russell H. "A Statistical Evaluation of Latin American Democracy," *Western Political Quarterly,* 9:607-19, 1956.

Floro, George K. "Continuity in City Manager Careers," *American Journal of Sociology,* 61:240-46, 1955.

Fogarty, Michael P. "Vocations of the Executive," *Social Order,* 7:130-34, 1957.

Fogarty, Michael P. and Hughes, H. Stuart. "Catholicism and Democracy," *Commentary,* 26:119-26, 1958.

Form, William H. and D'Antonio, William V. "Integration and Cleavage Among Community Influentials in Two Border Cities," *American Sociological Review,* 24:804-14, 1959.

Foskett, John M. "Social Structure and Social Participation," *American Sociological Review,* 20:431-38, 1955.

Freeman, Charles and Mayo, Selz C. "Decision Makers in Rural Community Action," *Social Forces,* 35:319-22, 1957.

Freeman, J. Leiper. "Local Party Systems: Theoretical Considerations and a Case Analysis" *American Journal of Sociology,* 64:282-89, 1958.

Freidrich, Carl J. "Creative Methods in Urban Political Change,"

Annals of the American Academy of Political and Social Science, 314:86-93, 1957.

French, J. R. P., Jr. "A Formal Theory of Social Power," *Psychological Review,* 63:181-94, 1956.

Fuchs, L. H. "American Jews and the Presidential Vote," *American Political Science Review,* 49:385-401, 1955.

Fusfeld, Daniel R. "Heterogony of Entrepreneurial Goals," *Explorations in Entrepreneurial History,* 9:8-18, 1956.

Gans, Herbert J. "The Sociology of the New Towns: Opportunities for Research," *Sociology and Social Research,* 40:231-39, 1956.

Geiger, K. "Changing Political Attitudes in Totalitarian Society: A Case Study of the Role of the Family," *World Politics,* 8:187-205, 1956.

Geiger, Theodor. "Sociology and Democracy," *Acta Sociologica,* 1:10-13, 1955.

George, A. L. "Prediction of Political Action by Means of Propaganda Analysis," *Public Opinion Quarterly,* 20:334-45, 1956.

Gifford, Ann. "An Application of Weber's Concept of Charisma," *Berkeley Publications in Society and Institutions,* 1:40-49, 1955.

Gilbert, G. M. "Dictators and Demagogues," *Journal of Social Issues,* 11:51-53, 1955.

Glantz, Oscar. "Class Consciousness and Political Solidarity," *American Sociological Review,* 23:375-83, 1958.

_____. "Protestant and Catholic Voting Behavior," *Public Opinion Quarterly,* 23:73-82, 1959.

_____. "Unitary Political Behavior and Differential Political Motivation," *Western Political Quarterly,* 10:833-46, 1957.

Glaser, W. A. "Intention and Voting Turnout," *American Political Science Review,* 52:1030-40, 1958.

Goffman, Irwin W. "Status Consistency and Preference for Change in Power Distribution," *American Sociological Review,* 22:275-81, 1957.

Golembiewski, R. T. "A Taxonomic Approach to State Political Party Strength," *Western Political Quarterly,* 11:494-513, 1958.

Gotshalk, D. W. "Politics and Civilization," *Ethics,* 66:79-86, 1956.

Grace, H. A. "A Quantitative Case Study in Policy Science," *Journal of Social Psychology,* 41:197-219, 1955.

Greer, Scott. "Individual Participation in Mass Society," in R. Young (ed.), *Approaches to the Study of Politics.* Evanston,

Ill.: Northwestern University Press, 1958.

_____. "The Social Structure and Political Process of Suburbia," *American Sociological Review,* 25:514-26, 1960.

Gusfield, Joseph R. "The Sociology of Politics," in Joseph B. Gittler (ed.), *Review of Sociology.* New York: John Wiley and Sons, 1957. Pp. 520-30.

Hacker, A. "Liberal Democracy and Social Control," *American Political Science Review,* 1:1009-26, 1957.

_____. "Political Behaviour and Political Behavior," *Political Studies* (Oxford), 7:32-40, 1959.

Haer, John L. "Social Stratification in Relation to Attitude toward Sources of Power in a Community," *Social Forces,* 35:137-42, 1956.

Hall, Harry S. "Scientists and Politicians," *Bulletin of Atomic Scientists,* 12:46-52, 1956.

Handlin, Oscar. "A Note on Social Mobility and the Recruitment of Entrepreneurs in the United States," *Explorations in Entrepreneurial History,* 8:1-5, 1956.

_____. "Do the Voters Want Moderation?" *Commentary,* 22:193-98, 1956.

Hanson, R. "Predicting a Community Decision: A Test of the Miller-Form Theory," *American Sociological Review,* 24:662-71, 1959.

Harris, Louis. "Some Observations on Election Behavior Research," *Public Opinion Quarterly,* 20:379-91, 1956.

Hastings, Philip K. "The Voter and the Non-Voter," *American Journal of Sociology,* 62:307, 1956.

Heberle, Rudolf. "Ferdinand Toennies' Contributions to the Sociology of Political Parties," *American Journal of Sociology,* 61:213-20, 1955.

Heimann, Eduard. "The Interplay of Capitalism and Socialism in the American Economy," *Social Research,* 24:87-113, 1957.

Higham, John. "The Cult of the 'American Consensus,'" *Commentary,* 27:93-100, 1959.

Himes, Joseph S. "Value Analysis in the Theory of Social Problems," *Social Forces,* 33:259-62, 1955.

Hoffman, Ross. "Conservatism," *Social Order,* 5:448-52, 1955.

Hofstadter, Richard. "The Pseudo-Conservative Revolt," *The New American Right,* ed. Daniel Bell. New York: Criterion Books, 1955.

Hook, Sidney. "Moral Freedom in a Determined World; Responsibility and Sentimentalism," *Commentary,* 25:431-43, 1958.

Hoover, Glenn E. "Political Parties in a Free Society," *American*

Journal of Economics and Sociology, 15:113-21, 1956.

Horowitz, Irving L. "The New Conservatism," *Science & Society,* 20:1-26, 1956.

Horowitz, M. W., and Perlmutter, H. V. "The Discussion Group and Democratic Behavior," *Journal of Social Psychology,* 41:231-46, 1955.

Hunt, N. C. "Pressure Groups in the U.S.A.," *Occidente,* 12:113-27, 1956.

Hunter, Floyd. "Studying Association and Organization Structures," in R. Young (ed.), *Approaches to the Study of Politics.* Evanston, Ill.: Northwestern University Press, 1958.

Huntington, S. P. "Conservatism as an Ideology," *American Politicial Science Review,* 51:454-73, 1957.

Jacobs, Paul. "Union Democracy and the Public Good," *Commentary,* 25: 68-74, 1958.

Jacobson, Norman. "The Unity of Political Theory," in R. Young (ed.), *Approaches to the Study of Politics.* Evanston, Ill.: Northwestern University Press, 1958.

Janowitz, Morris. "Social Stratification and the Comparative Analysis of Elites," *Explorations in Entrepreneurial History,* 8:6-11, 1956.

Janowitz, Morris and Delany, William. "The Bureaucrat and the Public: A Study of Informational Perspectives," *Administrative Science Quarterly,* 2:141-62, 1957.

Janowitz, Morris and Wright, D. "The Prestige of Public Employment: 1929 and 1954," *Public Administrative Review,* 16:15-21, 1956.

Jansson, J. M. "The Role of Political Ideologies in Politics," *International Relations,* 1:529-42, 1959.

Jewell, M. E. "Party Voting in American State Legislature," *American Political Science Review,* 49:773-91, 1955.

Kaberry, Phyllis M. "Primitive States," *British Journal of Sociology,* 8:224-34, 1957.

Kaplan, Abraham. "American Ethics and Public Policy," *Daedalus,* 48-77, 1958 (Issued as vol. 87, No. 2, Proceedings of the American Academy of Arts & Science).

Kariel, Henry S. "Democracy Unlimited: Kurt Lewin's Field Theory," *American Journal of Sociology,* 62:280-89, 1956.

Kaufman, Herbert. "Emerging Conflicts in the Doctrines of Public Administration," *American Political Science Review,* 50:1057-73, 1956.

Keefe, W. J. "Southern Politics Revisited," *Public Opinion Quarterly,* 20:405-12, 1956.

Kelsen, Hans. "Foundations of Democracy," *Ethics,* 66:1-101, 1955.

Kenkel, William F. "The Relationship between Status Consistency and Politico-Economic Attitudes," *American Sociological Review,* 21:365-68, 1956.

Key, V. O. "Secular Realignment and the Party System," *Journal of Politics,* 21:198-210, 1959.

——————. "A Theory of Critical Elections," *Journal of Politics,* 17:3-18, 1955.

Kimball, S. T. and Piersall, M. "Event Analysis as an Approach to Community Study," *Social Forces,* 34:58-63, 1955.

Kimbrough, Emory, Jr. "The Role of the Banker in a Small City," *Social Forces,* 36:316-22, 1958.

Klapp, Orrin E. "The Concept of Consensus and Its Importance," *Sociology and Social Research,* 41:336-42, 1957.

Klapp, O. E. and Padgett, L. Vincent. "Power Structure and Decision Making in a Mexican Border City," *American Journal of Sociology,* 65: 400-406, 1960.

Kling, Merle. "Towards a Theory of Power and Political Instability in Latin America," *Western Political Quarterly,* 9:21-36, 1956.

Koch, Adrienne. "The Status of Values and Democratic Political Theory," *Ethics,* 68: 166-85, 1958.

Kolko, Gabriel. "Economic Mobility and Social Stratification," *American Journal of Sociology,* 63:30-38, 1957.

Kort, F. "Predicting Supreme Court Decisions Mathematically: A Quantitative Analysis of the 'Right to Counsel' Cases," *American Political Science Review,* 51:1-12, 1957.

Lane, Robert E. "Elite Communication and the Governmental Process," *World Politics,* 10:430-37, 1958.

——————. "The Fear of Equality," *American Political Science Review,* 53:35-51, 1959.

——————. "Political Personality and Electoral Choice," *American Political Science Review,* 49:173-90, 1955.

Lang, Kurt and Lang, Gladys E. "Political Participation and the Television Perspective," *Social Problems,* 4:107-16, 1956.

——————. "The Television Personality in Politics: Some Considerations," *Public Opinion Quarterly,* 20:103-12, 1956.

Lasswell, H. D. "Current Studies of the Decision Process: Automation vs. Creativity," *Western Political Quarterly,* 8:381-99, 1955.

Lazarsfeld, Paul F. "Reflections on Business," *American Journal of Sociology,* 65:1-31, 1959.

Leiserson, Avery. "The Place of Parties in the Study of Politics,"

171

American Political Science Review, 51:943-59, 1957.

Levinson, Daniel J. "The Relevance of Personality for Political Participation," *Public Opinion Quarterly*, 22:3-10, 1958.

Levy, Marion J., Jr. "Some Aspects of 'Structural-Functional' Analysis and Political Science," in R. Young (ed.), *Approaches to the Study of Politics*. Evanston, Ill.: Northwestern University Press, 1958.

Lewis, Gordon F. "A Comparison of Some Aspects of the Backgrounds and Careers of Small Businessmen and American Business Leaders," *American Journal of Sociology*, 65:348-55, 1960.

Lipset, Seymour M. "Aristocracy in America," *Commentary*, 26:534-37, 1958.

——————. "Democracy and Working-Class Authoritarianism," *American Sociological Review*, 24:482-501, 1959.

——————. "Political Sociology," *Sociology Today*, eds. Robert K. Merton, Leonard Broom, Leonard S. Cottrell, Jr. New York: Basic Books, Inc., 1959.

——————. "Political Sociology, 1945-1955," in H. Zetterberg (ed.), *Sociology in the United States of America*. Paris, France: UNESCO, 1956.

——————. "The Radical Right: A Problem for American Democracy," *British Journal of Sociology*, 6:176-209, 1955.

——————. "Some Social Requisites of Democracy: Economic Development and Political Legitimacy," *American Political Science Review*, 53:69-105, 1959.

Lipset, Seymour M., Lazarsfeld, Paul F., Barton, Allen H., and Linz, Juan. "The Psychology of Voting: An Analysis of Political Behavior," in Gardner Lindsey (ed.), *Handbook of Social Psychology, II*. Cambridge: Addison-Wesley Publishing Co., 1954.

Long, Norton E. "American Business and American Liberals: Slogans or Responsibility," *Political Quarterly*, 29:166-77, 1958.

——————. "The Local Community as an Ecology of Games," *American Journal of Sociology*, 64:251-61, 1958.

Lorwin, V. R. "Working-Class Politics and Economic Development in Western Europe," *American Historical Review*, 63:338-51, 1958.

Lowe, F. E. and McCormick, T. C. "A Study of the Influence of Formal and Informal Leaders in an Election Campaign," *Public Opinion Quarterly*, 20:651-62, 1956-57.

Luce, R. Duncan and Rogow, Arnold A. "A Game Theoretic

Analysis of Congressional Power Distributions for a Stable Two-Party System," *Behavioral Science,* 1:83-95, 1956.

Manheim, Herman L. "Personality Differences of Members of Two Political Parties," *Research Studies* of the State College of Washington, 24:183-84, 1956.

Manis, Jerome G. and Stine, Leo C. "Suburban Residence and Political Behavior," *Public Opinion Quarterly,* 22:483-90, 1958.

March, James G. "An Introduction to the Theory and Measurement of Influence," *American Political Science Review,* 59:431-51, 1955.

——————. "Influence Measurement in Experimental and Semi-experimental Groups," *Sociometry,* 19:260-71, 1956.

——————. "Party Legislative Representation as a Function of Election Results," *Public Opinion Quarterly,* 21:521-42, 1956-58.

Marz, R. H. "The 'Democratic Digest': A Content Analysis," *American Political Science Review,* 51:696-703, 1957.

Matson, Floyd W. "Party and Faction: The Principles of Politics vs. the Politics of Principle," *Antioch Review,* 18:331-42, 1958.

Miller, Delbert C. "Decision Making Cliques in Community Power Structures," *American Journal of Sociology,* 64:299-309, 1958.

——————. "Industry and Community Power Structure: A Comparative Study of an American and an English City," *American Sociological Review,* 23:9-15, 1958.

Miller, Walter B. "Two Concepts of Authority," *American Anthropologist,* 57:271-89, 1955.

Miller, Warren E. "One-Party Politics and the Voter," *American Political Science Review,* 50:707-25, 1956.

——————. "Presidential Coattails: A Study in Political Myth and Methodology," *Public Opinion Quarterly,* 19:353-68, 1955-56.

——————. "The Socio-Economic Analysis of Political Behavior," *Midwest Journal of Political Science,* 2:239-55, 1958.

Mills, C. Wright. "Structure of Power in American Society," *British Journal of Sociology,* 9:29-41, 1958.

Mitchell, W. C. "The Polity and Society: A Structural-Functional Analysis," *Midwest Journal of Political Science,* 2:403-20, 1958.

Moore, Barrington, Jr. "Notes on the Process of Acquiring Power," *World Politics,* 8:1-19, 1955.

——————. "Sociological Theory and Contemporary Politics," *American Journal of Sociology,* 61:107-15, 1955.

173

Morgenthau, Hans. "Power as a Political Concept," in Roland Young (ed.), *Approaches to the Study of Politics.* Evanston, Ill.: Northwestern University Press, 1958.

Morris, G. "Democracy and Culture," *Ethics,* 66:87-91, 1956.

MacColl, J. E. "Public Attitudes to Politics," *Political Quarterly,* 30:6-17, 1959.

MacKinnon, W. J. and Centers, R. "Authoritarianism and Internationalism," *Public Opinion Quarterly,* 20: 621-30, 1956-57.

MacRae, Duncan, Jr. "Roll Call Votes and Leadership," *Public Opinion Quarterly,* 20:543-58, 1956.

McClosky, Herbert. "Conservatism and Personality," *American Political Science Review,* 52:27-45, 1958.

McCormick, Thomas C. and Wahl, J. Richard. "Predicting Election Turnout: A Test of a Behavior Hypothesis," *American Journal of Sociology,* 61:39-47, 1955.

McDill, Edward L. "Anomie, Authoritarianism, Prejudice and Socioeconomic Status: An Attempt at Clarification," *Social Forces,* 39-239-45, 1961.

McKitrick, E. L. "The Study of Corruption," *Political Science Quarterly,* 72:502-14, 1957.

Nadel, S. F. "The Concept of Social Elites," *International Social Science Bulletin,* 8:413-24, 1956.

Nettler, Gwynn. "Cruelty, Dignity, and Determinism," *American Sociological Review,* 24:375-84, 1959.

—————. "A Measure of Alienation," *American Sociological Review,* 22:667-77, 1957.

—————. Nixon, Raymond B. and Jones, Robert L. "The Content of Non-Competitive vs. Competitive Newspapers," *Journalism Quarterly,* 33:299-314, 1956.

Northrop, F.S.C. "What Kind of an American Civilization Do We Want?" *Annals* of the American Academy of Political and Social Science, 325:1-10, 1959.

Oliver, Henry M., Jr. "Attitudes toward Market and Political Self-Interest," *Ethics,* 65:171-80, 1955.

Oliver, W. Donald. "Rational Choice and Political Control," *Ethics,* 66:92-97, 1956.

Oppenheim, F. E. "Interpersonal Freedom and Freedom of Action," *American Political Science Review,* 49:353-63, 1955.

Parker, Hilda W. and Parker, Joseph P. "Democratic Principles in Social Problems," *American Journal of Economics and Sociology,* 16:369-78, 1957.

Parsons, Talcott. "The Distribution of Power in American Society," *World Politics,* 10:123-43, 1957. (Reprinted in his *Structure and Process in Modern Societies.* Glencoe, Ill.: The Free Press, 1960.)

Paul, Julius. "The Supreme Court: Mirror of the American Conscience," *American Journal of Economics and Sociology,* 19:1-15, 1959.

Pelligrin, R. J. and Coates, C. H. "Absentee Owned Corporations and Community Power Structure," *American Journal of Sociology,* 61:413-19, 1956.

Penniman, C. "Science and State Government," *Midwest Journal of Political Science,* 1:334-38, 1957.

Peterson, Helen L. "American Indian Political Participation," *Annals* of the American Academy of Political and Social Science, 311:116-26, 1957.

Petrie, C. "The Place of the Professional in Modern Diplomacy," *Quarterly Review,* 605:295-308, 1955.

Phillips, N. R. "The Conservative Implications of Skepticism," *Journal of Politics,* 18:28-38, 1956.

Pieper, J. "Knowledge and Freedom," *Review of Politics,* 19:147-54, 1957.

Plamenatz, J. "Electoral Studies and Democratic Theory: A British View," *Political Studies,* 6:1-9, 1958.

Polsby, Nelson W. "The Sociology of Community Power: A Reassessment," *Social Forces,* 37:232-36, 1959.

—————. "Three Problems in the Analysis of Community Power," *American Sociological Review,* 24:796-804, 1959.

Pool, Ithiel de S., Keller, Suzanne, and Bauer, Raymond A. "The Influence of Foreign Travel on Political Attitudes of American Businessmen," *Public Opinion Quarterly,* 20:161-75, 1956.

Porter, J. "Elite Groups: A Scheme for the Study of Power in Canada," *Canadian Journal of Economic Political Science* 21:498-512, 1955.

Powell, Inge B. "The Non-Voter: Some Questions and Hypotheses," *Berkeley Publications in Society and Institutions,* 1:25-35, 1955.

Prothro, J. W. "Verbal Shifts in the American Presidency: A Content Analysis," *American Political Science Review,* 50:726-39, 1956.

Press, C. "Voting Statistics and Presidential Coattails," *American Political Science Review,* 52: 1041-50, 1958.

Presthus, R. V. "Behavior and Bureaucracy in Many Cultures," *Public Administration Review,* 19:25-35, 1959.

Pye, Lucian W. "Communication Patterns and the Problems of Representative Government in Non-Western Societies," *Public*

Opinion Quarterly, 20:249-57, 1956.

Reiss, Albert J., Jr. "An Analysis of Urban Phenomena," in R. M. Fisher (ed.), *The Metropolis in Modern Life.* New York: Doubleday, 1955.

_____. "The Sociological Study of Communities," *Rural Sociology,* 24:118-30, 1959.

Reissman, Leonard. "Life Careers, Power and the Professions: The Retired Army General," *American Sociological Review,* 21:215-21, 1956.

Riemer, Neal. "Some Reflections on The Grand Inquisitor and Modern Democratic Theory," *Ethics,* 67:249-56, 1957.

Riesman, David. "Private People and Public Policy," *Bulletin of the Atomic Scientists,* 15:205, 1959.

_____. "Some Observations on the Limits of Totalitarian Power," in his *Individualism Reconsidered.* Glencoe, Ill.: The Free Press, 1954.

Riesman, David, and Glazer, Nathan. "The Intellectuals and the Discontented Classes," *Partisan Review,* 32:47-72, 1955.

Riker, William H. "The Paradox of Voting and Congressional Rules for Voting on Amendments," *American Political Science Review,* 52:349-66, 1958.

Riker, William H. and Schaps, Ronald. "Disharmony in Federal Government," *Behavioral Science,* 2:276-290, 1957.

Ringer, Benjamin J. and Glock, Charles Y. "The Political Role of the Church as Defined by Its Parishioners," *Public Opinion Quarterly,* 18:337-347, 1954-55.

Rosenberg, Morris. "Misanthropy and Political Ideology," *American Sociological Review,* 21:690-95, 1956.

_____. "Power and Desegregation," *Social Problems,* 3:215-23, 1956.

_____. "Some Determinants of Political Apathy," *Public Opinion Quarterly,* 18:349-66, 1954-55.

Rosenzweig, R. M. "The Politician and the Career in Politics," *Midwest Journal of Political Science,* 1:163-72, 1957.

Rossi, Peter H. "Community Decision-Making," *Administrative Science Quarterly,* 1:415-43, 1957.

Roucek, J. S. "Minority-Majority Relations in Their Power Aspects," *Phylon,* 17:24-30, 1956.

Rourke, F. E. "Secrecy in American Bureaucracy," *Political Science Quarterly,* 72:540-64, 1957.

Sartori, G. "Electoral Studies and Democratic Theory. A Continental View," *Political Studies,* 6:9-15, 1958.

Sayre, Wallace S. " 'Urbanism and Government, 1957-1977': A

Rejoinder," *Annals* of the American Academy of Political and Social Science, 314:82-85, 1957.

Sayres, William C. "Disorientation and Status Change," *Southwestern Journal of Anthropology*, 12:79-86, 1956.

Scammon, R. M. "Voting for President in the Larger Metropolitan Areas, 1952-1956," *Midwest Journal of Political Science*, 1:330-33, 1957.

Schein, E. H. "Brainwashing and Totalitarianization in Modern Society," *World Politics*, 11:430-41, 1959.

Schermerhorn, Richard A. "Power as a Primary Concept in the Study of Minorities," *Social Forces*, 35:53-56, 1956.

Schlesinger, Joseph A. "Lawyers and American Politics: A Clarified View," *Midwest Journal of Political Science*, 1:26-39, 1957.

——————. "A Two-Dimensional Scheme for Classifying the States According to Degree of Inter-Party Competition," *American Political Science Review*, 49:1120-28, 1955.

Schmidhauser, J. R. "The Justices of the Supreme Court: A Collective Portrait," *Midwest Journal of Political Science*, 3:1-57, 1959.

——————. "The Political Behavior of Older Persons: A Discussion of Some Frontiers in Research," *Western Political Quarterly*, 11:113-24, 1958.

Scholfield, F. A. "A Sociological Approach to Economic and Political Problems," *Federal Economic Review*, 4:48-63, 1957.

Schubert, Glendon A., Jr. "The 'Public Interest' in Administrative Decision-Making: Theorem, Theosophy or Theory?" *American Political Science Review*, 51:346-68, 1957.

——————. "The Study of Judicial Decision-Making as an Aspect of Political Behavior," *American Political Science Review*, 52:1007-25, 1958.

Schulze, R. O. "The Role of Economic Dominants in Community Power Structure," *American Sociological Review*, 23:3-8, 1958.

Schulze, R. O. and Blumberg, L. O. "The Determination of Local Power Elites," *American Journal of Sociology*, 63:290-96, 1957.

Seligman, Lester G. "Developments in the Presidency and the Conception of Political Leadership," *American Sociological Review*, 20: 706-12, 1955.

Shannon, Lyle W. "Is Level of Development Related to Capacity for Self-Government?", *American Journal of Economics and Sociology*, 17:367-82, 1958.

Sharp, Harry. "Migration and Voting Behavior in a Metropolitan

Community," *Public Opinion Quarterly,* 19:206-209, 1955.

Sheppard, Harold L. and Masters, Nicholas. "Union Political Action and Opinion Polls in a Democratic Society," *Social Problems,* 5:14-21, 1957.

Shils, Edward A. "The Concentration and Dispersion of Charisma," *World Politics,* 11:1-19, 1958.

_____. "The Intellectuals and the Powers: Some Perspectives for Comparative Analysis," *Comparative Studies in Society and History,* 1:8, 1958.

_____. "The Intellectuals, Public Opinion, and Economic Development," *Economic Development and Cultural Change,* 6:55-62, 1957.

_____. "Primordial, Personal, Sacred and Civil Ties; Some Particular Observations on the Relationships of Sociological Research and Theory," *British Journal of Sociology,* 8:130-45, 1957.

_____. "Intellectuals, Public Opinion and Economic Development," *World Politics,* 10:232-55, 1958.

Showel, Morris. "Attitudes Toward Conflicting Political Institutions," *Public Opinion Quarterly,* 20:604-12, 1956.

Sibley, Mulford Q. "The Place of Classical Political Theory in the Study of Politics," in R. Young (ed.), *Approaches to the Study of Politics.* Evanston, Ill.: Northwestern University Press, 1958.

Sinha, Durganand, 'Rumors as a Factor in Public Opinion during Election," *The Eastern Anthropologist,* 8:63-72, 1954-55.

Smiley, Donald V. "The Two-Party System and One-Party Dominance in the Liberal Democratic State," *Canadian Journal of Economic Political Science,* 24: 312-22, 1958.

Smith, J. M. and Cotter, C. P. "Freedom and Authority in the Amphibial State," *Midwest Journal of Political Science,* 1:40:59, 1957.

Smith, L. "Political Leadership in a New England Community," *Review of Politics,* 17: 392-409, 1955.

Smith, M. Brewster. "Opinions, Personality, and Political Behavior," *American Political Science Review,* 52: 18-26, 1958.

Snyder, Eloise C. "Uncertainty and the Supreme Court's Decisions," *American Journal of Sociology,* 65:241-45, 1959.

Snyder, Richard C. "A Decision-Making Approach to the Study of Political Phenomena," in Roland Young (ed.), *Approaches to the Study of Politics.* Evanston: Northwestern University Press, 1958.

_____. "Game Theory and the Analysis of Political Behavior," in *Research Frontiers in Politics and Government*. Washington, D.C.: The Brookings Institution, 1955.

Spindler, George D. "Education in a Transforming American Culture," *Harvard Educational Review*, 25:145-56, 1955.

Srole, Leo. "Social Integration and Certain Corollaries: An Exploratory Study," *American Sociological Review*, 21:709-16, 1956.

Stedman, M. S., Jr. "American Political Parties as a Conservative Force," *Western Political Quarterly*, 10:392-97, 1957.

Stephenson, T. E. "The Changing Role of Local Democracy, the Trade Union and Its Members," *Sociological Review*, 5:27-42, 1957.

Stokes, Donald E., Campbell, Angus, and Miller, Warren E. "Components of Electoral Decision," *American Political Science Review*, 52:367-87, 1958.

Suchman, Edward A., and Menzell, Herbert T. "The Interplay of Demographic and Psychological Variables in the Analysis of Voting Surveys," *The Language of Social Research*, ed. Paul F. Lazarsfeld and Morris Rosenberg. Glencoe, Ill.: The Free Press, 1955.

Sussman, Leila A. "FDR and the White House Mail," *Public Opinion Quarterly*, 20:5-16, 1956.

Swanson, G. E. "Agitation in Face-To-Face Contacts: A Study of the Personalities of Orators," *Public Opinion Quarterly*, 21: 288-94, 1957.

Tannenbaum, Percy H. "What Effect When TV Covers a Congressional Hearing?" *Journalism Quarterly*, 32:434-40, 1955.

Thompson, James D. "Authority and Power in 'Identical' Organizations," *American Journal of Sociology*, 62:290-301, 1956.

Tivey, Leonard. "The System of Democracy in Britain," *Sociological Review*, 6:109-24, 1958.

Tivey, L. and Wohlgemuth, E. "Trade Associations as Interest Groups," *Political Quarterly*, 29:59-71, 1958.

Toby, Jackson, "Are Polls Superior to Primaries for Determining a Party's Best Vote-Getter?" *Public Opinion Quarterly*, 20:717-18, 1956-57.

Trow, Martin. "Small Businessmen, Political Tolerance, and Support for McCarthy," *American Journal of Sociology*, 64:270-81, 1958.

Truman, David B. "The Impact on Political Science of the Revolution in the Behavioral Sciences," in *Research Frontiers in Politics and Government*. Washington, D.C.: The Brookings Institution, 1955.

Udy, Stanley H., Jr. " 'Bureaucracy' and 'Rationality' in Weber's Organization Theory: An Empirical Study," *American Sociological Review*, 24:791-98, 1959.

──────────. " 'Bureaucratic' Elements in Organizations: Some Research Findings," *American Sociological Review*, 23:418-20, 1958.

Warren, Roland L. "Toward a Reformulation of Community Theory," *Human Organization*, 15:8-11, 1956.

──────────. "Toward a Typology of Extra-Community Controls Limiting Local Community Autonomy," *Social Forces*, 34:338-41, 1956.

Warriner, Charles K. "The Nature and Functions of Official Morality," *American Journal of Sociology*, 64:165-68, 1958.

Watkins, Frederick M. "Political Theory as a Datum of Political Science," in R. Young (ed.), *Approaches to the Study of Politics.* Evanston, Ill.: Northwestern University Press, 1958.

Westley, William A. "Secrecy and the Police," *Social Forces*, 34:254-57, 1956.

Wilensky, Harold L. "The Labor Vote: A Local Union's Impact on the Political Conduct of Its Members," *Social Forces*, 35:111-20, 1956.

Williams, Robin M., Jr. "Unity and Diversity in Modern America," *Social Forces*, 36:1-8, 1957.

Wilson, F. G. "Public Opinion and the Middle Class," *Review of Politics*, 17:486-510, 1955.

Windmuller, John P. "Foreign Affairs and the AFL-CIO," *Industrial and Labor Relations Review*, 9:419-32, 1956.

Witte, Edwin E. "The New Federation and Political Action," *Industrial and Labor Relations Review*, 9:406-18, 1956.

Wood, R. C. "The New Metropolis: Green Belts, Grass Roots or Gargantua?" *American Political Science Review*, 52:108-22, 1958.

Wright, Charles R. and Hyman, Herbert H. "Voluntary Association Memberships of American Adults: Evidence from National Sample Surveys," *American Sociological Review*, 23:284-94, 1958.

Wright, Quincy. "The Peaceful Adjustment of International Relations: Problems and Research Approaches," *Journal of Social Issues*, 11:3-12, 1955.

Wrong, Dennis H. "The Perils of Political Moderation," *Commentary*, 27:1-8, 1959.

──────────. "The United States in Comparative Perspective: Max Lerner's *America as a Civilization*," *American Journal of Soci-*

ology, 65:499-504, 1960.

Zimmer, Basil G. and Hawley, Amos H. "Local Government as Viewed by Fringe Residents," *Rural Sociology,* 23:363-70, 1958.